Getting Real

Proven Strategies for Student Survival
and
Academic Success

Alicia Barbara Harvey-Smith

Duncan & Duncan, Inc., Publishers

For information or to contact the author, address correspondence to:

Duncan & Duncan, Inc., Publishers
2809 Pulaski Highway, P.O. Box 1137
Edgewood, MD 21040
(T) 410-538-5580 (F) 410-538-5584

Library of Congress Catalog Card Number: 97-67574

Harvey-Smith, Alicia Barbara
    Getting Real—Proven Strategies for Student Survival and Academic Success
        1. Academic Preparation 2. Study Techniques 3. Success
          Strategies 4. Self-Improvement

5 4 3 2 1

ISBN: 1-887798-02-1

Dedication

To My Divine Guide, Power and Glory Forever!

This book is dedicated
to tomorrow's leaders
in hopes that it will
inspire and educate.
To the littlest of all,
prepare and grow strong.

Brandi
Mica
Laura
John, III
Ashley
Carlisle, Jr.
Kirkland
Rachel
Lemar
Erica
Shawnna

"Carpe Diem"
Sieze the Day

Acknowledgments

Special Thanks to:

(Ma) Zelma M. Harvey for your continous support,
inspiration and encouragement.

Donald for your ability to generate wonderful insight
propelling me forward with love.

My brothers and sisters for believing in me and letting me know it,
Alice, Rufus, Yvonne, Lewis, Gregory, Gerald, and Carlisle.

Stephanie Bushrod Dunlap, a sincere and special friend.

Toby Ballard, an officer and a gentleman.

Virginia Hunter, a single parent making miracles happen.

Terry Felton, for your spiritual reflection and Kimberly June for your
technical skills and effort on the original manuscript.

To all of my teachers who freely shared and
evoked treasures from within.

For all things wise and wonderful, I give thanks.

Foreword

Upon meeting the Wizard of Oz, Dorothy and her companions presented their problems and ultimate needs for a "brain that can think, . . . a heart that can feel, . . . courage, . . . and . . . the comfort of home." The Wizard's response to them all was (and I take liberty in paraphrasing), "You have it already; the answer is within you."

"The answer is within you!" So simple a solution, yet so often difficult for many of us to accept and believe.

On a similar note—a usually accepted assumption is, that individuals destined for success take matters into their own hands. "No deposit, no return" may well be their battle cry, for it appears that early on, they discover that a long-term investment in patient, disciplined effort is required to meet personal goals.

Through this manual, the author attempts to convince students that they alone hold the key to their own academic success. The author suggests a feasible and immediate response to the problems of under achievement and unfulfilled goals—have the student assume some responsibility for his\her own success.

The bottom line, according to the author, is that successful students learn to develop a sense of where they are going and, they take an active part in both mapping and tracking the route.

While the author offers concrete suggestions and specific advice for dealing with daily situations and problems faced by students, she also introduces basic principles of success designed to guide students through the process of setting and realizing life goals. The presentation is direct and conversational, a reflection of the many encounters the author has had with frustrated, underachieving students.

This handbook is full of practical advice and sensible observations that will prove useful to many students, counselors, and parents alike. Having read the book once, the reader will not discard it but rather keep it as a handy reference to be used over and over again. The author leaves the reader with the subtle, but ever present reminder that *much of our destiny lies in our own hands!*

Dr. Rufus Sylvester Lynch
President, Center for Studying Social Welfare and Community Development, and current President of the PA Chapter, National Association of Social Workers

———Contents———

Opening Thoughts

"Small opportunities are often the beginning of great enterprises."

Demosthenes

Begin this book with these thoughts in mind:

- I am worth the effort.

- I will learn new ways of thinking and acting.

- I will focus on my success.

- I am part of a learning community, and will surround myself with others who seek success.

- I promise to support and learn from others.

- I will share my success with others by being an example of the best that I can be.

- I understand that striving for success is hard work. Three keys to achieving it are believing in myself and my abilities, and preparing myself. The feeling of success is one that I will want to experience time and time again.

• **I have everything I need within me to succeed.**

This book will explore your attitudes about studying and success, as well as reducing stress, building support systems and special advice for African-American Scholars, student athletes, parents and instructors. It will provide you with specific strategies which have been proven to work; however, you must practice each strategy. Success can be and will be yours if you prepare!

Begin each day with these thoughts . . . say each statement aloud.

I am a winner.

I can and will achieve.

I will prepare myself for success.

I will think, act, respond and plan as winners do.

I am a winner and it feels good!

Introduction

To the Student:

I believe in you, more than you will ever know. I know that you can achieve wonderful things; I know that you have the power to change the world one person at a time beginning with yourself.

Your reading this book is an indicator to me that you care about becoming the best student possible. This book is a step in that direction.

You are wonderful, unique and capable. I believe this. Learning, however, begins with what you believe about yourself.

Do you feel you are capable; do you feel confident in taking risks, or asking questions? These things are important to your success, no matter what your age.

Your commitment and determination play a big role in how high you will reach or how high you will soar. It's all possible, and it's up to you, but not you alone. Your parents, instructors, and others truly interested in your success also play a supporting role. Their role is important but not as important as yours.

No matter what your academic level is, this book has something for you. Students from middle school to graduate school and beyond have used these strategies and they work. I believe they will work for you.

You can accomplish anything that you plan and prepare for. The ability to study and retain information efficiently is a skill that can be mastered. Taking your learning to a higher level is my goal, by providing tools to boost and encourage your motivation and self-esteem.

The tips in this guide will help if you read them, believe them, and most important, use them. If you implement these strategies through conscientious practice time and time again, the sky will truly be the limit.

So remember, I believe in you and wish you the best always.

Getting Started:

Let's start by examining some beliefs that students have about learning. Do you have any of these beliefs?

Belief #1: If you haven't learned to study properly by now it's too late.

Fact #1: It's never to late to learn effective techniques. The key is to apply them.

Belief #2: If you had difficulty in high school, you should not consider college.

Fact #2: Many students improve considerably from high school to college.

Belief #3: Only nerds get good grades.

Fact #3: Any student who wants good grades, and prepares to get good grades, gets good grades.

Belief #4: Because you start college you will finish.

Fact #4: 40% of students entering college will not graduate when planned and many not at all.

Belief #5: Good grades in high school ensure success in college.

Fact #5: Good grades in high school are a good indicator, but don't ensure college success.

Belief #6: Gaining admission is the most difficult part of college.

Fact #6: Graduating can be much more difficult.

Belief #7: Instructors hate it when students ask stupid, unnecessary questions.

Fact #7: As a good student, it is your job to ask questions. No question should be considered stupid or unnecessary. If it will help you or clarify a point, go for it!

Don't forget that the purpose of this guide is to help you achieve success as you pursue excellence in school, college and life.

Here's to you and success—Making The Connection!

To Instructors, Parents, and Those Truly Interested In Student Success

Recognizing that we all have paramount roles to play in the transformation of student lives, I cannot over emphasize the importance of the impact that our interactions both in and out of the classroom has in influencing a student's beliefs about self. It is my contention that success begins with a solid and stable belief in self. With this in mind I encourage the reinforcement of a positive self-concept in preparing students for success.

Studies clearly indicate that effective student-teacher interactions are linked to long-term retention particularly in college. Being that this has been identified as one of the key factors influencing academic persistence, we must work to create a higher quality of interactions with our students.

As an instructor, it is vital to recognize and appreciate the diverse talents and experiences our students bring to the table. Knowing that each student has a great capacity to be taught as well as to teach, we must cultivate this ability and nurture its expression.

In appreciating our student's diversity, it is imperative that we view their varying cultures as both relevant and significant to their overall growth and development. The key to this is creating and fostering communities of inclusion within the classroom.

As we prepare students for learning we must pay attention to the total student. Holistic approaches to teaching and learning have been shown to increase both scholastic and academic retention.

One essential element to accomplishing this task is to actively and vigorously teach learning skills. This combined with empowerment and success strategies geared to improving fundamental belief systems will help students see their unlimited possibilities.

As a parent, I ask that you invest time with your student(s) helping them to understand the value of this material. Providing positive and consistent reinforcement, will also be important. Setting your expectations realistically, yet at a level that provides a challenge is essential. Students perform better when there is a balance in the challenges placed before them and the support that they receive to assist them to achieve.

This book hopes to blend these elements allowing students to achieve academic and motivational success. It strives at presenting these elements because, interestingly enough, a large number of educators view topics of academic preparation, study skills and goal setting as areas felt to need no real attention or emphasis within the day to day nucleus of classroom life.

Yet still, many parents believe that these very same skills are taught in school and in many cases, come naturally, leaving students on the other hand, short changed simply because they were never taught the basic skills involved in learning or how to become successful students. In essence, we hold them accountable for knowledge they have never appropriately received exposure to.

We can and must change this. Research also indicates that successful and unsuccessful students differ greatly in how they approach studying and academic preparation. These differences go far beyond motivation, or potential learning style preferences. Learning how to learn is as essential as learning specific content areas. Teaching students how to learn is vital.

In this rapidly changing, increasingly competitive world with exponential increases in technology and available information, life long learning is inevitable; increasing the level of this knowledge and the ability to apply it becomes keen. We who are interested in helping students navigate the waters of academics, play a critical role in the development of life long learning, and its overall quality.

It is paramount now more than ever, that we fully equip our students with the tools required for continued learning. This book will facilitate the process. It is a beginning of capitalizing at the highest level on our limited human resources. As pace-setters in a global economy, we must become a total learning society, valuing and educating each individual while developing, sharpening their skills and increasing their self-esteem. Learning how to learn cannot be left up to students alone.

It must be taught and supported in and out of the classroom. Together we can make their dreams reality by letting them see the possibilities within and giving them the prerequisite skills to bring out their best!

Alicia B. Harvey-Smith

Special Message for Athletes

Unleashing Your Secrets to Winning

As an athlete, you know how to win. You have been taught to develop a plan and to execute it. You know the importance of taking charge, being determined and most significantly, practicing. All of these things are equally as important as you plan to win in your classes and careers. By building upon your current techniques and using them academically, you will undoubtedly unleash true power in winning. By devoting the same drive, focus, and energy in the classroom that you use in competing in your chosen sport, you will excel.

To help you identify what makes you successful in your sport, try this. Make a list of things you feel make you a successful athlete.

1.
2.
3.
4.
5.

Once you understand your strengths and talents as an athlete, it will become easier to see how those same skills can be used in your classes, career and in other areas of your life.

We hear stories all the time about "the dumb jock." I have always failed to see why this occurs because, I believe "jocks" hold the real key to super success and achievement. I want you to envision and accept the idea of the "Jock as a Scholar." Athletes at all levels are achieving great successes by approaching their classes in the same way that they approach the big game.

Believe me, after putting in the effort and seeing your effort rewarded with a high grade, this matches the excitement and feeling of winning—scoring the winning point, or goal, hitting a home-run, running a touch down and crossing the finish line—no better feelings.

Studying and practicing are vital to being a successful athlete in sports. For example, many athletes, particularly football players, will review a game book or film daily to analyze the game. Using this same approach, daily review, to study your classnotes and assignments can only increase your knowledge and your grades.

Here are some suggestions that I have collected for student athletes which have helped them with their academic success.

1. Complete the majority of your studies at least 48 to 72 hours before a big test or presentation.

Reason:

Just like in sports, the most intense and difficult practices for a Saturday game occur on Monday, Tuesday, and Wednesday. The last two days are considered practice sessions or walk throughs.

2. Create your own practice test as you prepare for exams.

Reason:

It's like having a scrimmage or practice game prior to actual competition. Try it. Make your own test questions or use some other assignments or tests. Take your practice test throughout the week before your exam, specifically the two days prior to your exam. When possible, use the same environmental conditions that will exist during your actual test, particularly time limitations if they will exist.

3. Before your test, remember to study all material that you might have missed during your initial practice.

Reason:

Your approach should be the same as when you concentrate on any mistakes or areas in need of improvement after a scrimmage or practice game.

4. Relax, focus, concentrate, eat a healthy meal, and rest before your exam.

Reason:

This is vital to getting ready for a big competition.

Knowledge creates possibilities. As an athlete you are constantly increasing your knowledge about your skills and yourself. This knowledge involves learning and change. Adjusting to change and implementing new game plans are essential to your success. For you to be a champion, you must be a committed learner—one who is motivated and willing to do what it takes. Persistence, whether it's on the field or court, or in the pool or classroom, will pay off.

Cultivating the Habits of Champions

Respect the learning process. Set standards and aim high. It is also important that you respect your instructors and your classmates. You're all on the same team. Take your studies seriously. *Attend practice*—In other words, *go to class.* You can't win the game, if you're not in the game. It's worth the effort.

By utilizing the tips in this section, along with the other strategies contained in *Getting Real*, you will achieve the academic success that you desire. The "Jock as a Scholar" is already a reality and can be your reality if you approach the game of sports and the game of academics with their intellectual and physical challenges, with the same energy and concentration you use to approach athletics, you will win the game of excellence.

B efore beginning chapter one, take a moment to complete the abilities locator questionnaire. Use it as a way to start looking realistically at your current skills and attitudes toward your overall academic preparation.

This questionnaire was developed to show you where you might start in *Getting Real*. It's an opportunity to determine which study skills you need to develop or improve. Read each statement. If the statement applies to you, check true. If the statement does not apply to you, check false. See the end of the questionnaire for instructions on how to interpret your results.

The Abilities Locator Questionnaire

Part I. Establishing Realistic Goals and Using Reliable Support Networks

	True	False
1. I always set goals.	_____	_____
2. I have difficulty making decisions about my future.	_____	_____
3. I will work with a counselor to answer my questions when necessary.	_____	_____

	True	False
4. I know what is required to achieve my goals.	____	____
5. I review the progress I am making toward my goals periodically.	____	____

Part II. <u>*Active Listening and Note Taking Skills*</u>

	True	False
6. When I am listening to a lecture, I am easily distracted.	____	____
7. I know the words to listen for during class that will tell me what is necessary to write.	____	____
8. I never take notes during class.	____	____
9. When I take notes, I cannot keep up with the teacher.	____	____
10. I am able to remember parts of the lecture after class.	____	____

Part III. <u>*Managing Time Effectively*</u>

	True	False
11. I manage my time without difficulty.	____	____
12. I am frequently late for class.	____	____
13. I always have enough time to complete my assignments.	____	____
14. I organize my assignments to study according to deadlines.	____	____

15. There is never time for fun. _____   _____

Part IV. *Enhancing Memory and Concentration Skills*

	True	False
16. I never remember what I've studied well enough to pass tests.	_____	_____
17. I usually associate new material with what I already know.	_____	_____
18. I study in the same place each time.	_____	_____
19. I am easily distracted when studying.	_____	_____
20. I always ask questions in class.	_____	_____

Part V. *Applying Critical Thinking Skills to Reading and Writing*

	True	False
21. It is easy to relate what I read to my own experiences.	_____	_____
22. I don't see a purpose for what I read.	_____	_____
23. When I look at a word, I can usually recognize the meaning of its prefix, root, or suffix.	_____	_____
24. When I see an unfamiliar word, I often figure out what it means by looking at how it is used in the sentence.	_____	_____

	True	False
25. After reading, I create a plan for my writing.	_____	_____
26. I use a study system for remembeing key terms and definitions.	_____	_____
27. I am an active reader.	_____	_____
28. I never look for main ideas when reading.	_____	_____
29. I look for details that support main ideas and I underline or mark them.	_____	_____
30. It is easy to write a thesis statement and support it.	_____	_____

Part VI. *Reading Textbooks Effectively*

	True	False
31. I look the chapter over to see what it is about before beginning.	_____	_____
32. Textbooks are easy to read.	_____	_____
33. I am able to focus my attention on what I read.	_____	_____
34. I can read chapter headings and turn them into questions.	_____	_____
35. I am comfortable using a glossary.	_____	_____
36. I review the tables and other visual aids in chapters.	_____	_____

	True	False
37. I use mapping techniques to organize information.	——	——
38. I frequently underline in my textbooks.	——	——
39. I take notes from my textbooks to help me study.	——	——
40. I review my notes before and after class.	——	——

Part VII. *Improving Test Performance*

	True	False
41. I usually know what to study for tests.	——	——
42. I have a system for reviewing for tests.	——	——
43. Tests make me nervous.	——	——
44. If I don't know the answer to a multiple-choice question, I guess.	——	——
45. I always run out of time when taking a test.	——	——
46. I am easily distracted when taking tests.	——	——

Part VIII. *Improving Math, Science, and Literature Skills*

	True	False
47. I complete extra math problems at the end of the chapter.	——	——

	True	False
48. I know why I make the errors I make on my math tests.	____	____
49. I prepare differently for math and science than I do for other classes.	____	____
50. When studying a foreign language I use study guides and other charts to clarify.	____	____
51. I can determine the theme of a short story.	____	____
52. I am comfortable with using multiple science formulas.	____	____

1. Count the number of *false* answers for each section. If you have more than one per section, you may want to improve or develop the skills identified by the section heading.

2. If you have checked true to the majority of the questions, you may well be on your way to *Real Success*. Use **Getting Real** to help you achieve and maintain the success you desire.

   Prioritorize your sections according to the areas needing the most work; those with the greatest number of false responses and those which connect to your current goals, objectives and courses.

1

Your First Steps

Knowing that my best can only come from me, I accept myself just as I am.

Alicia B. Harvey-Smith

State Your Purpose

Clearly identifying and understanding your goals is probably the most important first step you will take in achieving measurable success for yourself. What are goals? Goals are simply the ambitions which you aim for; those things you wish to obtain or achieve. Have you ever heard the question, "If you don't know where you are going, how do you know when you have arrived?" Or, "If you don't know where you are going you probably won't get there." Goals are those things which allow us to clearly know where we are going. By mapping out a process and checking when we will most likely achieve what we planned is an important strategy. To achieve your goals you must be motivated. *Remember*, nothing is achieved without enthusiasm. Try this: state your goals. I want you to consider three immediate goals (goals you would like to accomplish within the next 2 years) and three long range goals (goals you plan to accomplish within the next 10 years).

List your immediate and long range goals.

Immediate Goals   Long Range Goals

_____   _____

_____   _____

_____   _____

Writing your goals down is essential. One is always more motivated when they have written their goals down and visualized them. Visualization will be discussed in a later chapter and is defined as the active ability to see yourself accomplishing a specific task. Making yourself put your goals on paper starts you thinking in the right direction. *Remember*, review your goals constantly and begin to note what things are necessary to achieve them. End goals (the final outcome like passing the class, getting a good exam grade) are made up of several smaller steps or process goals. Now that you have stated your goals and put them on paper, look at them and ask yourself are these goals realistic? Are they right for me? Are these my goals or someone elses goals? Your goals should be just that—your goals. Be careful not to set standards for yourself that will bring no joy in accomplishment. To thine own-self be true.

Set goals that make you happy. You can work to achieve excellence in those things under your control, and to which you have a true commitment. It is counter-productive to worry about what other people think or what their goals may be for you if you are not in agreement. If you continue to worry in this manner you are ultimately giving up control over your own life. This is a difficult but vital lesson to learn when it involves those we love. Remember that those we love, and those who love us have our best interest in mind and want us to be happy. Our true goals, and our enthusiasm toward achieving them is a reflection of our commitment and is directly tied to our happiness.

Take Control

Staying focused is a major key to keeping control of our goals. If you plan to achieve your process goals one by one, it is certain that you will achieve your end goal. Understand that realistic goals create opportunities for success. You will do your best by taking things one move at a time and staying in control by mastering the process goals—those steps necessary to accomplish the goal. An example of a process and an end goal would be completing medical school (the process) and becoming a doctor (the end goal).

Success depends largely on both process goals and end goals. This is where the journey begins. Taking the steps necessary to accomplish these goals is what puts you on top!

Organize Yourself

Guess what? The way you plan and use your time reveals a lot. The first thing that it reveals is how organized you are. I'd like you to think for a moment about what getting organized really means. Take a second and write it down. On that same piece of paper answer the following questions.

Getting organized means:

_____

_____

_____

1. Where, when and how do you study best?

Many students study best immediately following school or class; others need a break before going back to the books. Many students need a desk, still others work best at a table with a large surface area. A lot of students find it productive to listen to music and even have no difficulty with a TV on in the background. They claim it helps them to concentrate. Some like studying alone or with someone else. It's really important that you think seriously about what works best for you. Focus on your study habits, what could be improved and which behaviors can be changed now.

Organizing yourself helps you to be far more productive in less time. Let's find out how organized you really are. Ask yourself the following questions.

2. When do I learn best?
- immediately after class
- when I've eaten
- after a break
- early
- late
- other _____

3. How do I learn best?
- alone
- after rewriting notes
- when I'm with someone
- when I read or recite aloud
- when someone else checks my results
- other _____

4. Where is the best place for me to study?
- in my room
- in the basement/family room
- at the kitchen table
- at the library
- other _____

5. Ask yourself: Do I have different study habits for different subjects? Why do I study subjects in different ways? For example: Do you need to practice spelling words out loud? Do you need to underline phrases in English?

6. You should be striving to find out *what* you study best. Ask yourself: **What subjects are essentially the hardest for me?**

- Math
- Language
- English
- Science
- other _____

7. **Who can help me at school?**
    - instructors (be specific)
    - the Counseling Center (great for referrals, assistance with improving study skills and a friendly ear)
    - other students (be specific) _____

8. **Who can help me at home?**
    - mom or dad
    - siblings
    - neighbors
    - friends
    - partner(s)
    - other _____

Being organized is very necessary to secure academic success. Spending too much time playing at your computer, watching TV or listening to music will cause you some problems at test time. If you have trouble knowing what to study it becomes even more important to organize yourself.

Using a calendar to actually schedule the times of your classes and work hours will prove effective in mapping out and scheduling the appropriate study time. Your calendar will help you to visually see what demands are being made on your time. Not only can you map out and plan study and review time, but test preparation time specifically for each subject as well.

Remember: Organizing your time, study, space and life will be paramount in achieving academic success. Let's talk briefly about organizing your materials. Not understanding how to organize books, notebooks, worksheets and an assignment book can cause you as much frustration as not knowing how to organize your time.

Basic Tips for Organizing Your Materials

- If possible, use a different notebook for each subject, so your notes won't get mixed up.
- If unable to use a different notebook for each subject, try using a three ring binder with tabs for different subjects. Then all of your notes for all of your subjects will be in one place.
- Put the date on each page, then you'll know when you took your notes.
- Keep all papers your teacher/instructor returns. They will prove helpful in reviewing your tests and writing reports.
- Copy and file papers by date and subject at home.

You must organize your work area at home to stay on top. Even if you share workspace with others, your special area should be organized. If you have an organized work space it should:

- be available when needed
- be large enough to store materials needed
- have proper lighting/ventilation

Maintaining a special spot for studying becomes easier when you establish a routine and make daily checks on your materials. When you are organized, you will:

- know when it's your best study time
- know what subject you will need to plan extra study time for
- know where your best study spot is
- know where your materials are

• know when, each week, you will have time to study

• know what you need to study

Knowing all of this puts you in control. Review these pointers when preparing to study and make them a part of your routine.

Starting Tips

As mentioned previously, commit these startup tips to memory.

1. State your goals.

- Goals are vital to your success.
- Write them down and visualize.
- Map out each step it will take to achieve them.
- Stay focused and on course.
- Make sure your goals are your goals and no one elses.

2. Answer the following questions to help yourself.

- How do you study?
- When do you study?
- How frequently do you study?
- Where do you study?

Getting organized and staying organized is one of the most important steps you will take in securing success. It increases your productivity. Examine your study habits to make any necessary changes. It is extremely important that you organize your space and time to accommodate the demands being made in your life.

You are a Winner. This is the beginning of your journey!

Two key things that I will remember and use from this
chapter are:_____

_____

2

Mind Over Matter

Believe in yourself, your worth and your dreams. When you believe in yourself, you will positively reinforce those attitudes and actions which lead to positive outcomes. Take credit for all of you.

Alicia B. Harvey-Smith

Positive Reinforcement

As you continue toward achieving and maintaining academic excellence, I would like you to consider the following points:

To achieve the goals that you are setting you must be real and honest about those goals. In other words your goals must be clear, the steps must be clear and you must positively reinforce those behaviors which lead to success.

I would like you to remember that positive reinforcement is merely the practice of reaffirming an act or behavior; in this case, in a positive way. Everyone needs a little positive reinforcement. I believe that your primary reinforcement should come from your belief in self and your secondary reinforcement should come from the support systems that you build. We will talk more about support systems in a later chapter. For now, let's take an honest look at how to develop winning attitudes and beliefs. It's all in your mind.

There is a commonly held belief that what we think

determines largely what we do. A great deal of research by cognitive theorists, (people who study how the mind works) lend support to this belief.

I want you to expect to win, to achieve. Successful people always expect to win or succeed when they set goals or face a challenge. They know they can succeed and usually do!

Remember, if you think you can, or if you think you can't, you are right. Starting now, believe that you can, believe in yourself and make a real commitment to make your goals happen. You can do it when you think you can and prepare accordingly. When you do this, wonderful things happen.

Here are some examples of how to change your thoughts from negative beliefs to positive ones, as successful people do.

When you think unsuccessfully you:

- Anticipate failure
- Believe you can't
- Don't try
- Don't focus your efforts
- Give up

When you think successfully you:

- Anticipate success
- Believe you can
- Try hard
- Focus your efforts
- Never give up

Begin now to transform your thoughts, attitudes and behaviors to those which are successful, moving you to the attainment of your goals. Tap into the greatness within yourself and achieve your dreams.

Attitudes\Beliefs

What we think determines what we do.

Successful people face challenges with a mindset very different from unsuccessful people. The attitudes and beliefs that you are developing now will play a major part in the success you will achieve academically and in life. You must expect to succeed, prepare to succeed, try wholeheartedly to succeed, and dedicate, focus and commit your effort. The sky is the limit! Accept the greatness that lies within.

Identifying Success Models

Think of two successful people you know, and write four things about them which explains why you feel they are successful. Now, I'd like you to think of a successful experience you had in achieving a goal. What did you do? How did you feel? Hold on to that feeling. It's only the beginning.

List two successful people.

_____   _____

List four things which explain why you feel they are successful.

_____
_____
_____
_____

Write a successful experience you've had in achieving a goal.

_____
_____

What did you do and how did you feel?

_____
_____
_____

As we grow from children to adults we develop certain beliefs about ourselves. These beliefs are how we see ourselves and they help us to determine, in many ways, our place in the world. We often use our beliefs to predict whether we will succeed or fail. We develop beliefs in all areas of our lives. Sometimes, the beliefs we develop just aren't true. Many of these beliefs are based on messages we have received from others. These messages, I'll call scripts, constantly replay in our heads. If these scripts aren't positive, they may hinder your success.

Through practice you can change these negative scripts to positive ones. Here's how:

• Whenever negative thoughts creep into your head, reverse them immediately. For example: I'll never pass my math test, I'm too stupid (negative script).

• I'll prepare hard and pass my math test. It's always a challenge to me, but I can do it. (positive script).

Practice this activity to change your belief system. In time it will work.

Remember: Winners view problems as temporary challenges. They challenge any untrue belief they have.

Let's Practice!

List 4 beliefs you have about yourself in the following areas. What do you believe about your—

1. Abilities (how well you can do something)

   I believe: _____

   _____

2. Relationships (how well you interact/get along with others)

I believe: _____

_____

3. Appearance (how attractive you feel that you look)
I believe: _____

_____

4. Accomplishments as a student (how well you have achieved to this point)
I believe: _____

_____

Looking closer at the differences in the way a successful student looks at a challenge and the way a non-successful student may view the same challenge is demonstrated by the following:

Problem: my grades

Successful belief: I'll do better after I begin a new study routine.

This shows that the person views this as a temporary problem which can be controlled or solved through effort.

Unsuccessful Belief: All of my teachers hate me.

Remember: Successful beliefs motivate us to act and unsuccessful beliefs motivate us to do nothing.

Now I would like to introduce to you a concept which has been proven to aid individuals to think more positively about themselves, and build self-confidence.

Learn to Take Credit for Your Success

There is one thing stronger than all the armies in the world, and that is an idea whose time has come.

Assess your day and examine it for even small successes.

Acknowledge them and take positive credit. Taking credit is a natural, ongoing process. It helps one to understand that their efforts have led to their successes. By recognizing the importance of your efforts you will grow to learn that you have some control of your life, and through hard work you can achieve excellence. Taking credit is a first key step for anyone who dreams of success. It's an easy habit to develop if you follow this step by step process:

1. On a daily basis, review your successes both big and small.
2. Write them down each day.
3. Save them so that you can see the various challenges you've met.
4. Each day, help family, friends and classmates take credit for their successes as well! By helping them, you'll help yourself grow more confident and successful as well.

Remember: No one can truly help another without helping him or herself.

Let's Practice!

1. Write down any small or big successes you've experienced this week.

I am proud and take credit for the following successes:

_____

_____

_____

_____

Review these when you need encouragement and add to the list daily. Try it. It works!

Alicia's Secret Strategies to Success x 10

1. Plan to succeed—Set clear goals and map out the process for achieving them.
2. Work to succeed—Dedicate your energies to achieving.
3. Focus attention/effort on accomplishing goals—Commit yourself to your goals.
4. Seek active balance for success—Incorporate fun into your plans.
5. Seek out and use resources—Establish and use available supports.
6. Take credit for current successes and be proud of them. All successes count.
7. Recognize that each small success is a completed action moving you closer to attaining bigger successes. Appreciate the power of your success.
8. Try harder. Never give up—*Remember*, you can do it.
9. Think positively—Success starts in your mind.
10. Aim high—Our expectations guide our achievements.

Successful people have winning beliefs and attitudes. This chapter helped to expose you to some of the beliefs systems of successful people. Here is a list of *attitudes* which should be present in your planning and thinking.

- Positive belief expectancy - expecting the best from your efforts.
- Positive self-image - realistically seeing and accepting yourself.
- Positive self-control - your ability to focus efforts positively.
- Positive self-esteem - good beliefs and feelings about yourself.
- Positive self-awareness - being in touch with your strengths, weaknesses and dreams.

These attitudes will lead to specific outcomes:

- Desire to achieve.
- Positive self-motivation - self-direction/turn dreams to reality.
- Self-discipline - ability to focus effort, exemplifying high esteem.
- Self-projection - projecting a winning aura and personality.

If you can commit to these attitudes with zeal and enthusiasm the outcomes will lead to your academic success. Futhermore, they will help you acquire the elements necessary to be successful throughout life.

Two key things that I will remember and use from this chapter are:

_____

_____

3

Believing and Achieving

The people who get on in this world are the people who get up and look for the circumstances they want, and, if they can't find them, make them.

George Bernard Shaw

Accept yourself, don't lose faith. Accept all of your mistakes. When you don't, you will dwell on your weaknesses and focus on the imperfection of others. When you don't accept yourself, you dwell on past failures. Acceptance is a part of growth. Take a real good look at yourself. You're O.K.

Taking Stock—Self-Assessment

Conducting a self-assessment is a vital part of your growth and development. It entails looking closely at who you are. It's a way of examining your strengths and areas which may need improvement. At this stage of the game it's a vital step before you embark upon making changes; after all, if it's not broke don't fix it.

Self-assessments are useful in all areas of your life and help us to constructively criticize ourselves with the ultimate goal of self-improvement. The major theme of this book is possibilities. I believe that through concentrated effort, the required skills, attitudes and abilities can be acquired, and

that academic and personal hurdles can be overcome. Therefore, as we examine our strengths and areas which may
need improvement, keep in mind that these areas can be
strengthened, if you work to improve them. Answer the
following questions when conducting your self-assessment.

1. What are my strengths and weaknesses academically?

_____

_____

_____

2. What areas have I acheived well in, and not so well in?

_____

_____

_____

3. What subjects bring me the greatest level of enthusiasm?

_____

_____

_____

4. Am I motivated to achieve academically?

_____

5. Do I look for ways to improve myself?

_____

6. Do I respond well to constructive criticism?

_____

7. Am I willing to change habits that are not helping me
in order to achieve my academic goals?

_____

8. How hard am I willing to work to achieve success?

_____

_____

_____

9. What are my priorities as it relates to school, graduation and career choices?

_____

_____

_____

10. What sacrifices am I willing to make to achieve?

_____

_____

_____

Answer each question honestly. Save your answers. As you work through this book, your answers may change upon reflection. This assessment should help you begin to see yourself, goals, strengths and weaknesses more clearly.

Motivation/Determination

Now, that you have completed your self-assessment, compare the strengths with the goals you have chosen. Does there appear to be a relationship between what you desire to do and the strengths and abilities you expressed in the assessment. If not, let's begin to make some realistic adjustments. This does not mean to necessarily change your goals but to assess how you might realistically achieve them.

Another important component to your success will be your level of motivation and enthusiasm as well as your determination. In order to capture the success you desire, you must be able to motivate yourself enough to do the things required. For example, you might need to complete your assignments when you're not feeling up to it, in order to achieve academically. *Motivation* is that energy that comes from within which continuously propels you toward your goals. Nothing is ever done and done well without enthusiasm. Motivation will prove vital to your capturing and, most importantly, maintaining success. It may be that you are not highly interested in some of your courses or you may find that you are interested, but just can't bring yourself to do the homework, do to other pressures. The bottom line is that winners rise to the occasion and complete the necessary tasks.

Students who don't study as much as they should or don't do the necessary assignments typically feel guilty, which just usually makes matters worse by adding increased stress and anxiety. Lacking motivation is probably the most difficult *academic* problem a student can face. Prior to exploring specific techniques for improving study, let's focus our attention on how we might improve your level of motivation. Why do you want to complete school, graduate, and attend college? What are your motivations?

Much has been written about motivation and the role it plays in student success. All of the research simply points to one simple fact: that you must understand clearly what your goals are and your desired outcomes. In order to reach the desired goals or outcomes specific things *must* be done. Motivation comes when you really want to achieve a given outcome and are willing to do what is necessary; willing to sacrifice. Are you willing to pay the price for true success? Doing what it takes and giving what is required, are marks of commitment and determination to achieve. Do you have what it takes?

Centering/Positive Thinking

Centering and positive thinking can aid your motivation. The concept of centering is one that cannot be learned too soon. Centering is another technique which can be used to change the negative scripts we talked about earlier. Centering is a way of both balancing yourself and regulating your self-talk. Self-talk is that little voice inside your head that constantly monitors what you're doing, feeling, or thinking. It's like an internal coach, which can send both positive and negative messages. Positive self-talk, provides encouragement, praise, and good feedback. Positive coaching gets positive results. However, negative coaching is composed of criticism, anger, sarcasm and put-downs which lead to negative results. It also lowers ones confidence and self-esteem. Positive self-talk helps us to change the negative scripts we discussed earlier.

Your self-talk, the conversations you have with yourself should be positive, and filled with praise or constructive feedback. You must not put yourself down. If your self-talk is constructive, it can help you focus your attention. It can also assist you with concentrating. Many athletes use positive self-talk to focus and overcome adversity. If your self-talk is negative, change it by focusing on the positive. Your self-talk describes what you expect to happen. Everything you do happens in your mind first. Of course, stating it in your mind doesn't guarantee it, but it does increase the chance that it will occur. Use appropriate self-talk to guide your learning process. Learn where to focus your attention to perform your best. Self-talk focuses your attention inward reducing stress and anxieties allowing you to relax in order to succeed.

One way to learn to balance and center yourself, in order to focus your attention is by doing a deep breathing exercise.

Let's try it:

- take a deep breath
- count slowly 1,2,3 as you inhale
- let the air fill your lungs
- now exhale slowly
- concentrate on the way the air feels as your lungs push it out of your chest
- count 1,2,3 again while you exhale and let the noise and confusion flow out of your mind with the breath
- when you finished exhaling notice that you feel quieter and calmer

Centering works. It may take several breaths for you to notice that you have become more relaxed and focused. After practice it will have significant effects on your concentration. Use it to tune out negative self-talk before an exam or study period or when you just want to relax. In a later chapter, we will discuss other wonderful ways to relax and stay clear of anxiety.

Two key things that I will remember and use from this chapter are:_____

_____

4

Preparing for Excellence

No problem can stand the assault of sustained thinking.

Voltaire

Becoming an Active Learner

As a student, one major way to get the most out of your education is to get involved with it. You must take responsibility for your learning. What you will do in the future has a great deal to do with the choices you make now. After all, we are a compilation of all of our experiences both past and present. Therefore, what you do right now in preparing yourself, your level of interest, hardwork, and motivation is key to developing into the person you want to be.

Active learners are involved with their experiences. They are in the game. You can't win unless you are in the game. Active learners prepare for class, go to class, participate in class and assume some responsibility for learning. Being there is half the battle, be there.

Commitment to learning is vital and is demonstrated by total involvement in your educational experience. Unless you're willing to make this type of commitment, you're wasting your time. Suppose you have a bad teacher, or you feel you are not learning enough. You must still find a way to use your class time to your advantage. Are you asking questions, or attempting to work with your teacher?

Successful students learn coping skills which allow them to deal with boredom and frustration as well as difficulty and defeat. Thus, they learn to persist until they accomplish their goals. Give yourself a chance in class, be active. Many students are afraid of failing, or of asking stupid questions, or of giving the wrong answers. These types of fears and anxieties are normal. Just remember: There's no such thing as a stupid question, they're all important.

Usually there is more than one person afraid to ask the same question. So don't be selfish. By asking your question you're helping others too. Answering and asking questions in class builds confidence. Even if the answer is not a correct one, you took a chance which will lead to your growth. If you are quiet and passive in class, you may get by and may get a passing grade but is that *all* you want? I hope not. You deserve more. Sit close, not in the back of the room. Active learners maintain attention, focus on the instructor, stay awake, and avoid day dreaming.

Be more active in your learning. Take control. You can do it. Be determined to get the most out of class. Active learning, involves mental and physical adjustments which may keep you energized in and out of class. For example: A simple change in posture may keep you more alert. Sitting up, leaning forward and taking notes are all ways which help students stay focused on classroom lectures. Being a success academically requires a high level of energy, enthusiasm, alertness and involvement.

Another real benefit of active classroom learning is that your teachers/instructors will believe you're interested: *Remember*, instructors won't assume you're dumb when you make mistakes; they expect mistakes. Mistakes are an important and necessary part of growing and learning.

10 Tips On How to be an Active Learner

1. Take your seat in front of the class, not in the rear.

2. Sit up, lean forward and use active postures to remain alert.

3. Plan to ask at least one question per class session.

4. Highlight, outline, underline and take notes during class of relevant points.

5. Schedule at least one conference with your instructor to discuss papers, exams or just to talk. The instructor will be impressed.

6. Reward yourself for going to class and being active. This could be a movie on the weekend or any activity or treat you might enjoy.

7. When reading and you get drowsy, don't stop at once. Get up, shift positions, do more active tasks, or even go wash your face.

8. Do deep breathing exercises.

9. Be critical. Think of ways you can argue with the author of your text or come up with better examples (share examples with classmates/instructor).

10. Focus on your goals and how great you will feel once they are accomplished! Go for it!

Classroom Skills

Developing effective classroom skills are extremely important and will aid your overall success—helping you reach your end goals. Earlier in the chapter, I shared with you how important it is to be an active learner. At this point I'd like to give you some additional pointers on how to better handle yourself when talking to your instructors.

Many students experience anxiety just at the thought of

having to ask questions in class. Typically, students fear embarrassment from the reaction of their peers. Asking questions will clear up topic issues and improve test scores. It is equally as important to establish a comfort level with your instructors. You know what? Your instructors are human, and many of them have some anxiety with answering student questions. Instruction is a tough and important job. They are responsible for imparting and evaluating knowledge. Most are really concerned with doing well. Anxiety is a two way street. So relax. After the first few times the rest is a piece of cake, and will become easier.

Your classroom skills are very important to your success. Many students recognize that reading, writing, math and test skills are necessary in class; however, they often can't understand why other classroom skills are vital for their academic survival. It is very normal to be a little nervous or anxious when asking questions in class, or when having to approach your instructor. With practice and in time you will build greater confidence.

Here are some special tips which may help you become more comfortable with talking to your instructors.

1. Always ask questions—it's your job. It shows your interest and commitment.
2. Use positive thinking/visualization. It relaxes you and eases any fears. Use the positive self-talk we discussed earlier.
3. See your instructor after class or make an appointment to get your questions answered. If you set an appointment, show up!
4. Take time to write your questions down. This will help you focus on the issues you need clarified.
5. If at first you don't succeed, try, try again. If an encounter with an instructor doesn't go well, remember you're both only human; credit it as a bad day and go again.

What your instructor expects from you is probably not

real different from what you expect from them; a best effort, real concern and enthusiasm. In addition to that, the following five items would also rank high on their list of expectancies.

1. Maturity: Take your education seriously (Don't clown around in class.)
2. Attendance: Be there, no excuses
3. Promptness: Be on time, be prepared
4. Participation: Remember active learning
5. Complete assignments, adhere to deadlines. Don't ask for an extension unless it is absolutely necessary.

Dealing With Distractions

Dealing with distractions both in and out of class is a concern for many students. Sitting closer to the front will help elevate some of the classroom's external distractions or even centering deep breathing and active learning techniques will all prove useful, as previously discussed. Handling distractions at home or during study times is also an important challenge. Other major challenges which students constantly face dealing with distractions include such things as friends calling, invitations to go out, televisions, loud noises, sisters, brothers, and other interruptions. This is another instance where good concentration and your commitment will pay off. Your academic performance requires, as we mentioned earlier, accurate focus. One way to help yourself develop good concentration habits is by rewarding yourself when you have had successful periods of focused concentration, not allowing yourself to be distracted.

To do this you must set realistic goals for your time. Notice specifically what things are distracting you and avoid them when possible. Decide what places will provide the fewest distractions and work there. Ask your family and friends to help keep you on track by providing few interruptions. Distractions are an important obstacle for most students to overcome.This is a challenge, but not an impossible one. It requires that you organize your time, and prepare for intense concentration. It also requires the support of those who may be providing the interruptions.

External distractions are not your only concern. Internal distractions such as thoughts, songs and conversations in your head may also appear. Those scripts and self-talk we discussed earlier can cause quite an interruption when you attempt to focus. Simple deep breathing, or taking a breath or even changing to a different focus point will probably help, not to mention implementing a reward system when you have reached your goal of real and productive concentration.

Individual Success Plan

Developing an *Individual Success Plan* may provide you with the motivation to concentrate and avoid distractions, because it is a constant reminder of your goals, your strengths and the areas you wish to improve. It will help you to focus and affirm the goals you have set. There are a number of versions of success plans which you may use as a guide; however, I highly recommend that you develop your own. It is wise to share your plan with your parents, teachers, counselors and others who may provide you insight or who are supporters of your dreams. As you develop your Individual Success Plan, I'd like you to include some specific items to guide your planning and decision making.

The following format and elements can be used to get you started.

Individual Success Plan

Name_____

Date _____

1. My major strengths are:

_____

_____

2. My short-terms goals:

_____   _____

_____   _____

3. My long-term goals:

_____   _____

_____   _____

4. My educational goals:

_____   _____

_____   _____

5. My career objectives:

_____   _____

_____   _____

6. List steps necessary to achieve—

Short-term goals:

_____

_____

Long-term goals:

_____

_____

Educational goals:

_____

_____

Career objective:

_____

_____

7. The three things I enjoy doing most.

_____   _____   _____

8. The following people are my support system.

_____   _____

_____   _____

9. I affirm that I will persist to the completion of my goals. _____

10. I will utilize all the resources at my disposal.

_____

11. I am committed to my goals.

_____

This plan should be reviewed often and adjusted as your goals change.

Eleven Key Reminders

Commit to the following to achieve success.

In order to achieve my goals, I will:

1. Take the time to learn and understand what it takes to reach my goals by researching and asking others who know.

2. Focus and concentrate my effort to achieving my goals by creating a plan of action, detailing how I will accomplish them.

3. Avoid excessive distractions both internal and external by centering, relaxing and using self-talk.

4. Be committed, determined and motivated to achieve.

5. Organize my life to get the most out of my time and efforts.

6. Seek help from teachers, family and others when special problems arise.

7. Take responsibility for my learning by getting involved with my education through active learning.

8. Be flexible and understand that my goals may change over time.

9. Assess and be realistic about my strengths and areas needing improvement.

10. Learn from mistakes, and see them as opportunities for growth.

11. Continue to believe in my possibilities and strive to succeed in making my dreams reality.

Two key things that I will remember and use from this chapter are:_____

_____

5

Specific Strategies for Making the Grade

*Human perfection doesn't exist. Achievement requires prepa-
ration, excellence demands it. You can do it, but first want it,
plan for it and go get it! You have everything to gain.*

Alicia B. Harvey-Smith

How Learning Takes Place

L et's examine how learning takes place. Understanding
how information is processed and retained is essential.
Efficient and effective comprehension includes two major components: *input* and *recall*, the process of being able to remember what has been learned. We take in information in a
variety of ways. We take things in by seeing, reading, learning, listening, and doing. Taking in information is relatively
easy, the memory component of learning, also called retention, is not as easy.

For example; have you ever completed reading a page
and although you diligently read every word, once you finished, you couldn't remember a word? Well, it happens all
the time. You see, the key to real study and real learning is
to be able to remember what you take in from a text and
what you take in from a lecture or class discussion. What
about this, have you ever looked at your watch to see the time
and yet were unable to remember the time when someone asked

you immediately following? It's the same as reading a page and not remembering what you read. One of the fastest ways to learn something new is to relate it to something you already know. Honestly, that's how most learning occurs, by building a bridge between things we already know, knowledge we currently possess and new information. As a successful student, you should actively try to build these connections; the key is to always build on what you already know.

One effective way to remember information you read or hear is to attempt to *paraphrase it*. To paraphrase simply means to translate it into your own language, putting information or restating information in your own words. By paraphrasing you can stay active and alert. Research shows that by making these connections, and paraphrasing, learning is faster and more effective. A good way to test yourself is to attempt to restate, in your own words, the information your instructors are delivering. After restating, attempt to elaborate. Elaboration means to add details or expand your information. It speeds learning.

When you organize the material you're learning or paraphrasing, you are making learning permanent. Guess what? When you do this you are using your brain's extraordinary power to link or connect separate bits of information into a knowledge map, allowing you to locate and retrieve vital information. The process of building all of those connections is another example of elaboration. The purpose of any elaboration is to save time by making recall easier. How efficient you are depends on your elaboration skills and the type of material. You can create your own methods of elaboration; remember it is any method you use to help build connections between what you already know and what you are trying to learn.

Paraphrasing and organizing are the two most popular methods. Try these methods to improve your performance.

Concentration Skills

To be a winning student, how well you concentrate is

very important. Concentration means paying attention, focusing your thinking on what you're doing. This is how it works: you concentrate while reading—to follow the writer's ideas, you concentrate during class—to get the speaker's points, you concentrate while writing—to select the right words, and you concentrate while studying—to retain (remember and recall) information.

You can improve your concentration if you know what causes you to lose it. What causes poor concentration? Do any of the statements below apply to you?

• I'm easily distracted when I study.
• My mind wanders when I read.
• I can't seem to find time to study.
• I put off studying frequently.
• My mind goes blank on a test.
• If I don't like the instructor; I lose interest and don't pay attention.
• If the subject doesn't relate to what I really want to do, I have a hard time concentrating on it.
• If an assignment takes too long or is difficult, I usually don't stick with it.
• I don't have a career goal or reason to study.
• It's hard for me to listen and take notes at the same time.

After identifing some of the causes of poor concentration, you can now work to eliminate them. As I shared with you in an earlier chapter, you should also strive to eliminate distractions, be they internal or external. You may not be able, as you know, to eliminate all external distractions, but you can change how you might respond to them to stop them from interrupting your concentration. For example, ask friends not to call during the time that you plan to study.

You can also eliminate some internal distractions if you anticipate your needs. Use these tips:

• prior to studying, be sure that you have eaten and are rested.

When studying:
  - Be comfortable.
  - Make sure you understand the assignment.
  - If you are ill, postpone studying.
  - Avoid negative feelings and thoughts, they cause stress (when you have these thoughts, stop studying for a minute, take a break).
  - If you lack interest/motivation, study with a partner, someone who is interested and motivated.
  - *Remember*—to create a study environment (your own work area).

I want you to create a personal study environment, a place where you can study, review, and reflect without interruption. Do your studying when your concentration is at its peak.

When setting up your study area, pay close attention to lighting. Too little light will hurt your eyes. If the temperature gets too hot, you'll feel drowsy and sluggish. Cooler temperatures keep you alert. In terms of furniture, the key is comfort. Also, make sure you have all the supplies you need in your work area, as well as motivational aids. Display your calendar. Make your area creative and alive with energy. Keep a record of grades, confirming that your studying is paying off. Try these study strategies to eliminate distractions and improve concentration:

1. Break up large assignments, such as research papers, into smaller tasks, making them more manageable.
2. Study difficult assignments first when you have greater energy.
3. Separate similar subjects to break up any monotony.
4. Take breaks to rejuvenate.
5. Reward yourself.
6. Study from your own materials, utilizing parapharasing and other skills.

While you are reading, if you should discover that your

mind sometimes wanders, try this before starting :

1. Decide on your purpose for reading.
2. Turn headings and subheadings into questions to answer as you read.
3. Underline key ideas, words, and phrases.
4. Summarize key ideas in the margins.
5. Look up any word you do not understand.

Memory Skills

Here are twenty techniques to aid your memory. These are fun! Try them.

1. *Learn from the general to the specific:* Skim your assignments for the general idea before attempting to zero in on specifics. Step back, get the big picture, then the details will be clearer.

2. *Make it meaningful:* Know what you want from your education. Look for real connections between what you want and what you are studying. When information helps you to achieve something you want, trust me, it's easier to remember.

3. *Create Associations:* The data stored in your memory is arranged according to a scheme or pattern which makes sense to you. When learning new information link it (as we discussed earlier) to information you already know.

4. *Learn it once, actively:* There is an old saying which states, "People remember 90% of what they do, 75% of what they see, and 20% of what they hear." What does this mean? Well, action helps it stick. Learning takes energy! Test this theory by approaching your next study session with the same energy you take to the dance floor or basketball court. *Try this:* Sit up, on

the edge of your chair as if you are ready to spring or sprint forward or try standing up when you study. It's harder to fall asleep in this position. Some say their brains function more efficiently when they stand. Also, try pacing back and forth and gesturing as you recite material out loud. Use your hands. Get your whole body involved in studying. The techniques also help defeat boredom. Come on, be like NIKE, and just do it!

5. *Relax:* Did you know that when we relax, we absorb new information quicker and recall it with greater accuracy. (Relaxation techniques will be discussed in a later chapter) Relaxation is a state of alertness, free of tension. You can be active and relaxed!

6. *Create pictures:* Use your imagination. Draw diagrams and cartoons to connect facts and illustrate relationships. Relationships in abstract concepts can be seen and recalled when visualized. The key is to use your imagination. Visual information is associated with a different part of the brain than verbal information. When you create a picture of a concept, you anchor the information in two parts of your brain. This increases your chances of recall.

7. *Recite and repeat:* When you repeat something out loud, you anchor the concept in two different senses. The combined results are synergistic. The effect of using two different senses is greater than the sum of their individual effects. Saying it out loud and repeating it is key. Learning is more effective when voice and volume are used to trigger the brain. Repetition works because it blazes a trail to the brain, making information easier to recall. Repeat a concept out loud until you know it, then say it 5 more times.

8. *Write it down:* Writing helps you remember an idea.

Don't write it once, write it many times. Writing engages a different kind of memory than speaking. It prompts us to be more logical and complete.

9. *Reduce interference:* A little quiet goes a long way. Turn off or at least turn down your stereo or TV to study. Preferably find a quiet place free from distractions and for those of you who like a little distraction (i.e. music, etc.) keep it to a minimum.

10. *Use daylight:* Study your most difficult subjects during daylight. Many people can concentrate more effectively during the day; early hours can be especially productive. Some may find evening study hours work best for them. The quiet of late nights has proven particularly productive for me.

11. *Overlearn:* Pick your subject, examine it, add to it, and go over it until it becomes second nature. This technique is especially effective for problem solving.

12. *Strive for long term memory:* Short term memory is different than the kind of memory needed during exam week. Short term memory rarely last more than several hours. A review within minutes or hours of a study session can move material from short term to long term memory.

13. *Distribute learning:* Marathon study sessions are not effective. You can get far more done in four two hour sessions than in one 7 hour session. Break be tween sessions and study related or even unrelated topics to keep your interest up!

14. *Beware of attitudes:* (Remember, think like a winner) Don't let your attitude defeat you. If you believe math is difficult or boring, you probably will have difficulty with it. One way to defeat this atti

tude is to relate the subject to something you are interested in or your ultimate goal.

15. *Select what not to store in your memory:* Decide the essentials to be remembered. Base this on class lectures and notes. Extract key concepts.

16. *Combine memory techniques:* The combination of the techniques discussed intensify recall. Choose two or three to use on a particular assignment.

17. *Remember something related:* When you are stuck and can't remember something, stop and try to remember something related to it. Try brainstorming to jog your memory. Jot down as many answers as you can possibly think of.

18. *Notice when and how you remember:* Memory styles vary. Some people recall information best that they have heard, some recall what they read, and still others recall what they have seen or done. To develop your memory, notice when and how you recall information the easiest.

19. *Use it before your lose it:* The information stored should be used. It becomes more difficult to recall it when it hasn't been used. Read it, write it, speak it, listen to it, apply it and you won't lose it.

20. *Remember you never forget:* Adopt an attitude which exudes confidence, one that says I never forget. Support your attitude and belief with affirmations and positive self-talk.

Other real tips to improve your memory power:

• Actively decide to remember it.
• Visualize it.

- Remember key words related to it.
- Memorize it.

Now that you know that you can remember and retain more than you ever thought you could, and that you can use a few of the memory aids, as many students do, now you can make your recall even better. Let's take some time now to learn just a few more tips on acquiring a better memory by looking at it in different terms. The way I figure it, you can never have too much information on improving your memory.

Memory can be broken down as reception, retention and recollection. Because I want you to be the very best student you can be, here are some specific tips for accomplishing improvements with these three areas.

How to Improve Reception

- Pay attention/observe/stay focused.
- Use as many of your senses as possible to receive information. Look at the speaker; listen attentively and take notes.
- Ask questions because you can't recall what you don't understand.
- Before reading a chapter, survey or review it to get an overview of its content and establish your purpose.

How to Improve Retention

The key to retaining academic information is to make a conscious effort to remember.

- When using your text, underline and mark key points.
- Look it over frequently; review helps tremendously.
- Say it aloud—you're a successful student, and you're proud. Reciting improves retention. Recite from note-cards, texts, and study guides. This will activate your auditory senses and blaze new pathways to your brain.

• Do all of your assignments. It's good practice. It helps you internalize information. And after all, practice makes perfect!

How to Improve Recollection

Has this ever happened to you? You are taking a test, but you can't seem to remember an answer even though you know you know it. Only when the test is over, do you remember it.

• Before a test, organize the information you want to study (as I said earlier). Make it meaningful to you.
• Make summaries, or set up categories in which you group similar items.
• Figure out how you learn best. If it is visually, make diagrams, charts, or maps, and picture these in your mind as you study or test.
• Create your own practice tests. Anticipate test questions and answer them.
• Review old tests, and go over material that gave you trouble in the past. Past mistakes provide important clues for improvement.

Elaboration Techniques

1. *Paraphrasing*: Change terms, concepts, ideas or phrases into your own words.
2. *Organizing*: Put terms and concepts together in a chart, diagram or list in a manner that helps to explain the connections between terms and concepts.
3. *Mapping:* Organize facts or ideas, by their relationships to each other.
4. *Playing Instructor:* Imagine yourself having to teach the concepts to a friend. Practice asking, and answering questions in your own words.
5. *Imagery:* Form mental pictures or images to de-

scribe concepts. Use the pictures to clarify ideas before starting to link terms together. *"A picture is worth a thousand words."*

Memorizing has long been a technique students have used successfully to recall information. Learning becomes far more meaningful when you elaborate.When you combine memorization and elaboration, you get meaningful learning. Meaningful learning brings comprehension, the ability to understand and articulate that which has been learned.

A large number of students rely on memorization to learn something but do not necessarily understand it. They may memorize when they must remember material but don't have the time or motivation to understand it. However, as a successful student, your goal should be to make these moments rare. This type of learning is called *Rote*. *Rote* learning is the process of using your brain as a camera or machine, in that, a camera does not have to understand what's being copied. If you must use a rote technique to remember information that can't be connected to things you already know; use mnemonic strategies.

Mnemonics are tried and true systems. There are many mnemonic systems, and one of the most popular simply involves listing terms you want to remember, taking the first letter of each word to make up a name, phrase, or story. Try this as an example: What are the colors of the rainbow? Roy G. Biv = Red, Orange, Yellow, Green, Blue, Indigo and Violet. Now you try. Another fun way to use mnemonics is to use rhymes such as "i" before "e" except after "c". The key to using your memory more effectively is to realize that your brain never loses any data it receives. The information you collect remains with you always. Short of injuries or illness you can recall any information stored. I would like you to review the following memory techniques to help you design a fun and creative system for you which will take in to account your specific learning style. What follows will help you determine your learning style and include tips on understanding your instructor's teaching style.

Determining Your Learning Style

Understanding and using your learning style is another important key to securing academic success. You are an individual with very special and unique gifts. One of your unique qualities is how you choose or prefer to learn. By knowing your learning style, you unlock the easiest and most satisfying way you learn. Your learning style is automatic. When you are in a classroom environment that matches your style, it feels good. It feels right but in an environment that doesn't match, you will probably feel out of sync, out of place, uncomfortable and unable to do your best.

To assist you when you are in an uncomfortable classroom environment, you must learn your style and adapt to it in order to fit the environment and ensure success. Your learning style has many components. Which mode best fits your style?

Visual - "You have to see it."
　　　You learn best by reading or watching.

Auditory - "You have to hear it."
　　　You learn best by hearing.

Tactile - "You have to feel it."
　　　You learn best by touching, manipulating objects or by using your hands.

The teaching modes used can be visual, such as demonstrations, diagrams on boards or assigned readings; they can be auditory such as lecture or tapes, or they can be tactile, like a hands on activity. The best teaching occurs when there is a blending of modes to accommodate the varying learning styles. When the instructional mode is different from your preference, you must work harder to compensate. It takes more effort to concentrate. Let's determine your preferences with the following activity which is designed to help you determine your true learning style. Take an honest look.

What are your preferences?
(Check all that are true for you!)

1. I learn best by reading alone.   _____
2. I love lectures.   _____
3. I enjoy outdoor activities such as camping or
   sports.   _____
4. I like demonstrations.   _____
5. Class discussions are beneficial.   _____
6. I love to type and use computers.   _____
7. Illustrations, charts, and diagrams improve my
   understanding a lot.   _____
8. I'd rather listen to the instructor's explanation
   than do the assigned reading.   _____
9. I get more out of labs.   _____
10. Manuals and printed directions help me.   _____
11. I like audio cassettes of lessons/exercises.   _____
12. I prefer to work with machines and equipment
    than listen to or read explanations.   _____
13. I can do anything if someone shows me how.   _____
14. I follow directions best when they are read to
    me.   _____
15. It's not enough to show me; I've got to do it
    myself.   _____

Statements 1,4,7,10 and 13 are signs of a visual learner. Statements 2,5,8,11 and 14 are signs of an auditory learner. Statement 3,6,9,12 and 15 are signs of tactile learners. If your checks are spread evenly among two or more categories, you may be equally comfortable using one or more of the modes discussed. The way your body reacts to your classroom environment or your home study environment is also important. You should constantly listen to your body for clues. Determining your physiological preferences and building your schedule accordingly is another way of using your learning style to your advantage.

As we have discussed before, most people have a peak time of day when they are most alert and energetic. Throughout the day, your concentration, attention, and energy levels fluctuate. In the morning you might be alert and ready for anything, but as the day progresses, your energy decreases. If you learn to accept what you can not change, then you can adapt to situations that don't meet your preferences. The next activity will help you understand how your body's reactions might affect your ability to learn.

How does your body react?
(Check all that apply)

1. I am most alert in the morning. _____
2. I don't "come alive" until afternoon or early evening. _____
3. I'm most alert at night. _____
4. I concentrate and work best in bright light. _____
5. Bright lights are really distracting. _____
6. I need an adjustable lamp for lighting. _____
7. I am strongly aware of the classroom temperature. _____
8. I can't work or concentrate if the room is too cold or too hot. _____
9. I get chilled next to a fan, air conditioner or open window. _____
10. If my chair or desk in class is uncomfortable, I can ignore it and concentrate. _____
11. If my chair is not the right height, I become extremely uncomfortable and ache. _____
12. If I feel ill; I just can't think. _____
13. I can ignore being hungry or tired long enough to keep my attention on my work. _____
14. Mild feelings of illness usually don't distract me from my work. _____

Your answers indicate the following about your body's reactions. The time of day you are most alert, 1,2,3; your lighting preferences 4,5,6; your temperature preference 7,8,9; your comfort in relation to furnishings in classroom 10, and 11;

the extent to which hunger, fatigue and illness effect your ability to concentrate in class 12,13, and 14.

Remember: Your learning environment is far more than just a place where your class meets. How is your class structured? Is it traditional with desks in rows and the instructor directs all activities or is it non-traditional in structure with desks in circles and some student facilitation. All of this matters in shaping your educational experience. As a successful student you will have to adapt to whatever learning environment is available; however, knowing about your preferences will help you adapt more efficiently.

In an earlier chapter, we talked about how important your level of motivation is to your success. It is a key component. When your attitudes are combined, be they positive or negative, towards your goals, classes, and instructors, they may increase or decrease your opportunity for success. Many of your feelings about these issues will depend on your "locus or control." Locus means place; your locus of control is where you place responsibility for control over your life. Do you believe you are in charge? Do you believe others have complete control over what happens to you?

As a student, it can greatly affect your motivation. Let's examine where you place your control and how it can be used to help you become more successful. *What is your locus of control? Check only the statements that apply to you.*

1. When I can do the work, I can earn a good grade in any course no matter how bad the teacher.   _____

2. If the teacher isn't a good speaker or doesn't keep my interest, I probably will fail.   _____

3. I have the power to control what happens to me.   _____

4. I have no control over what happens to me.   _____

5. When I make a mistake, it's usually my fault.   ____

6. When I make a mistake, it's usually because someone didn't explain what I was suppose to do.   ____

7. My grades reflect how much I study.   ____

8. My grades aren't affected by the amount of studying I do.   ____

9. I can adapt easily to change.   ____

10. Adapting to change is difficult for me.   ____

11. When I fail a test, it's because I didn't study or understand the material.   ____

12. When I fail a test, it's because the test was unfair or the instructor didn't cover the material.   ____

13. I rarely need anyone to push me or make me study.   ____

14. I can't seem to make myself study.   ____

15. I am self motivated.   ____

16. I need someone to motivate me.   ____

If you checked mostly odd-numbered statements, you may have an internal locus of control. If you checked mostly even-numbered statements then you may have an external locus of control. *Let me explain.*

The internal locus of control

Students in this area can see the connection between the effort they put into a course and the grades they receive. These students tend to be self-motivated and positive thinkers. They believe that they can do whatever they set out to accomplish. They are not afraid of change. They welcome challenges. When they make mistakes, they can trace it back to something they did wrong or did not understand. They don't believe soley in mere luck or fate. They are in charge of their lives. When things go wrong, they try to figure out what they can do to fix it.

The external locus of control

Students in this area cannot see the connection between the effort they put into a course and the grades received. They believe teachers play favorites or award grades on the basis of personal feelings. Sometimes they believe that grades are the result of luck. They tend to be negative thinkers, needing others to motivate them or give them a push. They may also believe that many of the things they want in life are out of reach or that others are holding them back. They are afraid of change and prefer familiar routines.

When mistakes are made, they blame others for being unfair or for not giving them the right information. They believe they have little control. When things go wrong, they feel there is nothing they can do about it. Research clearly shows that locus of control affects achievement. The more internal your locus of control, the greater your chances for success. Thinking positively about yourself and your abilities, accepting responsibility for motivating yourself, and believing that doing your best will produce results is vital for success. Here are some great tips for helping you to develop more of an internal locus of control:

    1. Become a positive thinker.

    2. Accept responsibility for motivating yourself.

    3. Accept the fact that success results from effort.

4. Start listening to your self-talk.

Sharpening Your Thinking and Study Skills

Do any of the following statements sound like *you?*

1. "I study but I don't make the grades I want".
2. "I study a lot but I often study the wrong things".
3. "I read everything I'm supposed to; I just don't understand it."
4. "Even when I think I have learned something, I might not remember it".
5. "I have trouble concentrating".
6. "I never seem to have enough time".
7. "My textbooks are boring".
8. "I can always depend on my instructor to include a question I didn't study".
9. "This time I really must get organized."

These statements illustrate frequent concerns encountered by students. Sharpening your thinking and study skills is another vital key for securing your academic success. Knowing how to study helps you apply your knowledge and use your skills so that you will be successful. Learning style, thinking skills and study skills overlap. Thinking is the means by which you make sense of the world around you. The learning and activities you will be involved with will require critical thinking.

Critical thinking will help you make decisions, solve problems, reason logically, and use your creativity as well as process information. The following chart shows how thinking and study skills work together to help you with assignments you may be asked to do. These simple tips will prove very helpful as you plan and progress academically! Try them!

Thinking Skills	Tasks	Study Skills
Decision Making	Decide what to study	Set up a schedule
	Decide what's important in a chapter.	Find main ideas and key terms.
	Select courses.	Know requirements and use resources.
	Decide what to study for a test.	Review notes and assignments.
Problem Solving	Learn how to solve equations.	Use note cards to record sample problems.
	Learn composition of compounds for a chemisty test.	Use note cards to record formulas.
Logical Reasoning	Write a speech.	Make an outline.
	Follow a writer's ideas in a chapter.	Look for a pattern of organization.
	Relate to writer's ideas.	Make a chart or information map.
Processing Information	Read a chapter from a book.	Preview, underline, and make notes.
	Listen to a lecture.	Use listening and note-taking skills.
	Read test directions.	Use test-taking strategies.
Creativity.	Compose an orginal poem, drawing, song, essay or story.	Keep an "idea" journal or notebook.

Adapting to Your Instructors' Teaching Style

You know adjusting your thinking and behaviors to achieve success is hard work, but it is definitely worth the effort. This next area will cover some strategies you might use to adapt to the various teaching styles you will encounter. Just as you have a learning style, your instructors have their unique teaching style. You must adapt to the various styles your teachers use in order to be successful in their classes, as they should make adaptions to adjust to yours.

An instructor's teaching style largely determines the method of instruction he or she prefers. There are a large number of teaching styles; however, let's focus on the two primary types: *independent* and *interactive*. Each of these styles represent an extreme of behaviors.

The instructor whose style is *independent* is usually formal and businesslike with students and places far more importance on individual effort than group effort. This instructor will expect you to assume responsibility for learning to work independently, and to seek help when needed. Lecture is the preferred method of instruction. He or she will call on students to answer questions rather than ask for volunteers. Students in this instructor's class may feel competitive. If you feel comfortable in lecture courses and like working independently, you may be able to do your best work with an instructor whose style is independent.

The instructor whose style is *interactive* is usually informal in his or her relationships with students. Importance is placed on group effort and less on individual effort. The interactive instructor wants students to assume responsibility for learning but doesn't expect it, or leave it to chance.

This instructor will guide students through tasks step-by-step, and anticipate their need for help. Small group activities and large group discussions are the preferred methods of instruction. Rather than call on students, he or she will usually ask for volunteers to answer questions. Students may feel cooperative in this environment. If you feel most comfortable in classes where students do most of the talking and if you would rather work with others than by yourself, you may do your best work in an interactive classroom.

If you do not like or get along with one of your instructors, you may be reacting negatively to his or her teaching style if it is different from your learning style. ***Remember:***

maintain a winning attitude. Don't let your personal feelings keep you from being a success. Focus on those things you can do to meet the instructor's expectations, and attempt to adapt to his/her style. Concentrate on using all the strategies you are learning to master skills and concepts. If you make this effort, it will make a dramatic difference.

To analyze an instructor's teaching style, complete the checklist that follows. Fill in the name of one of your courses, then check each phrase that describes your instructor.

Course:_____ Instructor:_____

1. Formal, structured attitude   _____

2. Informal, casual attitude   _____

3. Encourages competition among students   _____

4. Encourages cooperation among students   _____

5. Primarily lectures to class   _____

6. Usually holds class discussions   _____

7. Emphasizes the importance of individual
    effort   _____

8. Emphasizes the importance of group
    effort   _____

9. Usually uses visual aids   _____

10. Seldom uses visual aids   _____

11. Calls on students   _____

12. Asks for volunteers   _____

13. Expects students to ask for help   _____

14. Guides students step-by-step   _____

15. Primarily focuses on facts   _____

16. Frequently shares personal experiences   _____

17. Tells what to do, gives directions   _____

18. Shows what to do, gives directions   _____

Odd-numbered items describe the *independent* teaching style. Even-numbered items describe the *interactive* style. If you checked more even-numbered than odd-numbered items, your instructor's style is probably interactive. If you checked some even-numbered and some odd-numbered items your instructor's style may be *independent* and *interactive*.

Two key things that I will remember and use from this chapter are:_____

_____

6

Planning Your Work

"People forget how fast you did a job, but remember how well you did it."

Howard Newton

Study Smart

Over the next several pages, I will attempt to provide specific tips on how to study. This section is very important because it should serve (as I hope the whole book will) as a resource which you can call on for future reference. Throughout each section, please take time to look at your study habits honestly. Looking at how you are currently studying, and looking at your level of motivation, will help you to make important progress.

As a successful student, and based on information provided in earlier chapters, I am sure you recognize the importance of developing a schedule. It is the most important thing that you can do to organize your life. There are major benefits to developing a schedule. The primary benefit will be to allow you to be more productive with your time. When developing your schedule remember the following *pointers*:

1. Design it to fit your class hours.
2. Block out ample time to study; a general rule is two hours study time for every hour in class.

3. Leave enough time to fit in other activities (study groups, etc.).
4. Vary the amount of time allotted based on the course and its current demands.
5. Post your schedule in a place where you can easily refer to it. Stick to it.
6. It is also very important to spread your study time out, so as to decrease the likelihood of the loss of concentration or the tendency to cram.
7. Schedule a review of classnotes as soon as possible after each class. (This works wonders.)

Studying smart involves dedicating your time and using it wisely. By establishing routine study periods in your study area, you will concentrate and focus better. This sets the stage for your improved performance. As a successful student this is one of the best habits you should strive to develop.

Attending your classes is a must. Being there is half the battle, and good attendance is one indicator of a good student. It shows you take your classes seriously. During your initial classes find out how the course is organized and how you will be graded. This will help you to devise an individual student success plan for the course (this plan was discussed in chapter 4). Basically it will answer: *What will you need to do to be successful in this course?* It will include such things as materials needed, number of sessions, grading system, and course expectations.

Remember these success tips for studying smart!

- To be a good listener, pay attention, sit up and get involved.
- Being a good listener and taking good notes go hand in hand.
- Taking good notes from lectures is an art that develops through practice.
- Use active learning in class, and out of class, ask

questions and exchange ideas with your classmates; two heads are usually better than one.

Learn the five R's of notetaking:

- <u>Recording</u>: Write it down. You may want to rewrite your notes from class. It helps reinforce the material.
- <u>Reducing</u>: Summarize. Put it in your own words. It helps you remember.
- <u>Reciting</u>: (remember this?) Just say it loud. Saying it aloud helps you sort out the material and improves recall.
- <u>Reflecting</u>: Think about it. Reflect on the assignment objectives and content.
- <u>Read</u> it over again and again and again.

More Tips on Studying Smart

The art to efficient studying involves your motivation, your personal efficiency, organization and your ability to strengthen your skills over time. There are several study systems which you can use to improve your overall performance. One of the most popular systems was developed by Francis Robinson of Ohio State University involving five major components: Survey, Question, Read, Recite, and Review or simply SQ3R. This method allows students to improve their study habits. Let's break it down and examine each component.

When You Survey a Textbook

To survey is to look over what you are doing before doing it. It's looking before leaping. First look at the whole book. Read the introduction and preface. Look closely at the contents page. Do this more than once. Leaf through the book, glance at headings and illustrations. This will help you become more comfortable with the text and how it's organized.

When You Survey a Chapter

Use the same approach, look it over first. Look closely at headings and sub-headings. Check out their order. This helps with sequencing when studying.

Question

Ask questions. It's your job! A large part of learning involves questions. As you study, read, review, and continuously ask yourself questions. There are two approaches to asking questions. One is to determine your questions and the other is to determine the author's questions.

Read

Reading provides the details necessary to master the material. It fills in the blanks. You should read in a manner that involves you with the material as if in dialogue with the author. Stay alert, as you progress through the text. Look for details, base them on the ultimate purpose of the text or chapter. Note important terms; look for italicized, boldfaced type. If you see this repeat it to yourself and make sure that you know what it means.

Checking Out Graphs, Tables and Illustrations

Read them. Read everything. Don't skip tables, graphs or diagrams. A simple picture can tell you what a whole section is about. They're also helpful in triggering your memory for future tests.

Recite

This is a natural. It's one of the oldest ways of learning. Your *aim* should be to recite for comprehension and recall.

Reciting for Recall

This is an excellent way of keeping your reading active. Recitation is an effective study method because it forces you to read actively and reveals things you don't understand immediately. If you recite, you can correct yourself on the spot.

Reciting is recalling. Stop as often as you need to and try to recall what you just read. The general rule: *as you read, stop in intervals to recite the substance, in your own words, of each major section in the chapter.* Research has shown that the earlier you recite (early in the chapter or text) the less you forget later on. The amount of time you spend reciting depends on what you are studying. It also keeps you attentive and the amount of time it takes appears far less than it is. This is a technique that is well worth the effort.

Review

Reviewing is vital. Try these quick reviewing strategies. Use them frequently, not just when preparing for exams. Once you have surveyed, questioned, read and recited, you are ready for reviewing. Always survey the material to be reviewed. This is done to refresh your memory. Recite before and after you read. Use your notes to guide your reviews. Review consistently before exams. A good old pre-exam review is also advised. Underlining and highlighting are special techniques used by successful students. Follow these tips to assure that you don't hit or miss haphazardly important issues.

1. Survey the reading first; do not underline or highlight.
2. Don't underline or highlight whole sentences.

As your questions are answered or you spot the main idea and important details, make a check mark in the margin. During the next reading, read specifically for the main idea, details and terms. At this point, underline or highlight. Many of the words in a sentence that contain an important idea are unimportant. Leave them out when you underline. Underline only the words and phrases which are essential.

Taking notes from your text is one way to be active in the learning process. Just write it down as *"what the author says."* By doing this, you make it part of your study power.

Methods of Outlining

- Use what ever clues the author provides.
- Use headings to form outlines.
- Convert headings into sentences.
- Organize your outline.

Winning Notetaking Ideas From Text

- Notes should contain main ideas and important details.
- Use enough information to trigger your memory later.
- Write legibly.
- Use summaries: Read them within your chapter and text and write them to explain what has been read and understood.

Time Management

The ultimate key to your success may be how well you manage your time. I have shared in other chapters its importance, but I want to take time here to emphasize the necessity of planning wisely. Time is a valuable resource; treat it as a treasure. At this time I would like to share some specific tips on how you can make the very best of your time allowing you greater efficiency and of course productivity. Time management for many students is seen as a means of control and restriction. It is sometimes viewed negatively. You should understand that if used appropriately and with planning you should be able to do all the things you want to do.

Effective time management will give you a chance to use your most valuable resource in the way you choose. In addition to the tips provided in earlier chapters, utilize the following suggestions when planning your schedule.

- Schedule fixed blocks of time first; start with class time and work time.
- Include time for errands.
- Schedule time for fun, stay balanced.
- Set realistic goals.
- Allow flexibility in your schedule.
- Avoid marathon study sessions.
- Set clear starting and stopping times.
- Always plan for the unexpected.

A fun way to take control of your time and organize your effort is to use a method I developed, which I call **OPEN**.

O—Establish realistic *objectives* or goals.
P—*Prioritorize* tasks and *process* steps needed to achieve your goals.
E—*Evaluate* how you use your time, look for the gaps.
N—*Now* make any necessary changes to get the most out of your time.

Another way of looking at it would be in order to manage your time effectively just *OPEN it!* Purchasing a calendar to use throughout the academic year is a smart idea. It will allow you to see at a glance what you need to accomplish each month, week or day to accomplish your course requirements and your goals.

As a successful student, you should begin the habit of writing lists of things to do and appointments to keep. Keeping a daily list can be a quick and easy way to start planning your time efficiently. This list should include whatever you want to do or whatever you need to remember that you might otherwise forget.

A major hurdle for many would be resisting the temptation to <u>procrastinate</u>. (Procrastination is simply needlessly postponing things that need to be done, until a later time.) Many times those things we postpone never get done.

Though some procrastination once in a while won't hurt, if you continue to delay your studies, or put off important assignments too often you will certainly sabotage your efforts to succeed.

Research has found four major reasons why people procrastinate. Perhaps you put off key assignments for one of these reasons also.

1. Your tasks appear difficult or time consuming.
2. You have difficulty getting started.
3. You lack motivation to do the assignment.
4. You are afraid of failing.

Putting off difficult or time consuming assignments makes them even harder to do when you get started and this further ensures that you won't be able to do your best because you will not have enough time. Try this: break a difficult task into smaller manageable parts that you can handle in short periods of time.

Learning to manage time and avoiding procrastination requires work on your part. Don't be discouraged if your initial efforts are unsuccessful. Keep trying. With practice you will get on track and stay there. Eventually you will take real control of your time and your life. Here are some tips to get you started:

1. Remember to divide a large assignment or project into smaller units of work that you can complete in one sitting.
2. Plan rewards for yourself for completing each part of the assignment. Do something you enjoy.
3. Make a schedule for completing a long assignment. Set a goal to spend a certain amount of time working each day until the assignment is finished.
4. Get organized. Your attitude toward studying will, in time, improve if you have an orderly work area with everything you need at your fingertips; books, pens, pencils,and paper so that you can begin the moment you sit down.

5. If you put off assignments because you do not know where to start or aren't sure how to do the work, find out exactly what you need to know. Make an appointment with your instructor, share with him or her your difficulty and ask for advice. If you have begun the assignment share your progress with the instructor. You could also talk to someone in your class. If you missed a lecture or have gaps in your notes, your friends might be able to fill you in.

6. Assume an attitude of confidence. Instead of thinking, "This is too difficult" or, "I'll never finish this." Be positive and think, "I can do this, if I get started right now," and, "There's a lot of work to do, but if I can do a little bit at a time, I'll be finished before I know it."

Real Tips for Finding Time When None Exists

• When you are finished with your studies or reviews, complete one more task before you quit. Start another assignment; then you will be ahead when you sit down to study the next time.

• Carry note-cards and other study materials with you so that you can make better use of *open time* or free time that normally gets wasted. Recite from your notes while you are in the car or on the bus, waiting in the dentist's office, standing in line, and walking to and from classes.

• When you have trouble getting started, select a specific task, such as seven pages of a reading assignment, and say to yourself, "I'm going to spend thirty minutes on this non stop." At the end of that time, review to see how much you've done. If you still aren't satisfied, complete thirty minutes more. A task may seem easier to complete if you are looking at thirty minutes of concentrated effort instead of several hours of unspecified work.

• Do two things at once. Combine recitation and review with another activity. Recite terms and definitions while you are jogging or walking. Review your notes while you are eating lunch.

Tips for Top-Notch Notetaking

Taking notes during class helps you to remember what the instructor said. Your notes will help you study later. Many students have used the following strategies and have gained control over their studies.

1. Get *ready* before the instructor starts class. Have materials ready. Put everything else away.
2. Keep your mind on what the instructor is saying. Try not to look at or think of anything else.
3. Write down the topic of the material as soon as the instructor says it.
4. *Listen* for important ideas the instructor says. Then, *write them* in your own words.
5. Is the information you're hearing new to you? If it's not new, you probably don't need to write it down.
6. Only write a few words or phrases to help you remember the information.
7. You don't need to write unimportant words, such as *the*, *a* and *is*. These words do not help you understand information better.
8. Use abbreviations or codes to help you write faster. (Here are some suggestions)

e.g.	for example
w/	with
w/o	without
@	about, at
re:	regarding, about
etc.	et cetera, and so forth
=	equals
b/c	because
b/t	between

Note: Use your outlining skills to take notes. *Remember*, they don't have to be perfect.

Rewrite your notes the same day you take them. Rewriting helps you organize better. It's also great for learning and remembering the information.

Listen for these and other key words from your instructor. *"One factor"; "Another thing"; "There are three ways to do this"; "Finally"; "An important point is"; "Remember";* etc.

Listen to your instructor's voice. Louder words are often important to write down and remember.

Now, let's see an example of notetaking. Suppose you hear this information:

"Today, we are going to talk about things that can help you study. First, think about the time of day you study. Study at your own best time: right after school, at night after dinner, or early in the morning. Next, decide where you'll study. Maybe you can find a quiet place where no one will bother you. Last, organize your work area. Make sure all of your materials are in one place. Then, you won't have to keep getting up for things you need. I'm sure you can use these suggestions to help you study."

If you had taken notes, they would look something like this:

A. Things to help my studying

   1. Best time of day
   2. Best place
   3. Organize materials in work area

Taking good notes will be absolutely vital to your academic success. One key reason for taking notes is to have the information available at some later time. It is also better to keep your notes in the most useful format possible, to help improve your review and achievement on tests.

In the following section, I recommend a notetaking format, which is a series of guidelines for taking notes in class. I believe these guidelines will help to make you not only a competent notetaker, but a successful student as well.

How To Take Good Notes In Class

Materials..............Three ring binder with dividers, notebook paper, one manila folder for each class, pens with erasable ink if you wish, hole punch.

Preparation Before..Read assignments, do homework, learn spelling and definitions of new vocabulary words, try to understand major concepts. Bring any preparation notes to class with you.

Preparation In........ Sit near the front of the classroom. Be sure you have a clear view of the instructor and the blackboard or viewing screen. Avoid classroom distractions.

Layout of Notes..... Leave left-hand 1/3 of page blank except for headings (just like this example). This leaves space for notes and comments when you review your work. In upper right hand corner put course name, date and page number. You'll need this if your notes are dropped or become unattached.

Writing Notes.........Write your notes in ink on one side of the paper only. Use your best handwriting even if it hurts. If you must doodle, do it on scrap paper. You want a crisp, clean copy that will be a legible.

Shorthand..............Make use of common symbols and abbreviations to make your notetaking faster and easier. Combine the following symbols with those shared earlier. Together, they will give you a wealth of abbreviations to add to your notetaking arsenal.

Shorthand Ex..........& (and)

ex. (example)

** (important)

... (and so on)

+ (plus or positive)

- (minus)

Q (question)

A (answer)

ASAP (as soon as possible)

ETA (estimated time of arrival)

ITP (initial treatment plan)

IEP (individual education plan)

Taking Notes..........Listen attentively first, then capture the important points. Your most important task is to hear and comprehend the lecture.

Do's.....................Do take notes from blackboard or viewing screen. If the instructor goes through all this work, then the material is important and will probably be on a test. Do take notes on discussion and when students ask questions. This Q & A exchange may clarify the lecture, but most students don't take notes when other students speak.

Questioning..........When you don't understand what your instructor is saying, don't interrupt, but do ask a Q ASAP. If you don't understand what is being said at the time, chances are you won't get what's coming next. Be brave, ask. You want your notes to make sense. Remember, there will be a test.

Clarify Notes........Review your notes ASAP after class. You may be able to augment, expand and clarify them. If you discover problems, check with your instructor.

Expand Notes.......Within 24 hours sit down with your notes and text. Check new words, formulae, equations, etc. from your notes with the text. Annotate your notes in the left margin as needed. Cross reference notes and text by writing text page in notes and note page and date in text. This will save you loads of time during test preparation.

Additional Help.....See your instructor during office hours if you are having difficulty with any of the material. If that doesn't solve the problem go to your campus tutoring service, or to a student who has done well in the course.

Save Your Notes...One last important point deserves to be made in favor of good notetaking. You may need your notes later in other courses. Many introductory courses provide basic information which is used as a basis in advanced courses. If your notes are well done, you can always use them again if you have forgotten basic information. This approach beats going through your old textbook chapter by chapter again.

Listening Skills

Many students, even the most successful ones, have difficulty listening to lectures from time to time. Effective listening is a necessary skill which can be improved over time, with practice. Do you have difficulty listening to lectures or deciding what is important to write in your notes? How about distractions or losing your place or does your mind wander into daydreams or other fantasies? Exams and other class activities are based on information presented in lectures, your ability to listen and take notes is closely linked to how well you do in class.

It is vital that you develop listening and notetaking skills that will enable you to gain as much from lectures as possible. Now in order to develop these necessary skills you must first decide to be, as I have stated earlier, an active participant instead of a passive recipient in the classroom. I truly believe that through continued practice, planning, faith and dedication you can achieve your goals. You must make a commitment to learn and assume responsibility for the outcome of every course by mastering these five essential tips for improving your performance.

1. Assume that you can get new knowledge from every lecture.
2. Attempt to follow the instructors' ideas.
3. Listen for key words.
4. Consider the views and questions of others in the class.
5. Listen attentively even when you are bored or don't agree.

Become An Active Listener

An essential component for classroom success is active listening. Since lecture\discussion is the preferred style of most instructors, you probably spend most of your class time listening.

There are two kinds of listeners—those who are *passive* and those who are *active*. Passive listeners do more hearing than listening. They are aware that the instructor is speaking, but they aren't making sense of what he or she says. Passive listening is a characteristic of the external locus of control. Passive listeners tend to expect instructors to motivate them and to interest them in the topic.

Active listeners pay attention to what they hear and try to make sense of it. Active listening is a characteristic of the internal locus of control. Active listeners tend to be self-motivated, and they expect to find their own reasons for being interested in a lecture topic. The chart below compares traits of active and passive listeners. Which kind of listener are you?

Passive Listeners	Active Listeners
Expects a lecture to be uninteresting.	Expects to will find something in the lecture of interest.
Assumes that information in a lecture will not be useful or pertainent.	Assumes that information in a lecture will be useful.
Looks for and is distracted by weaknesses in the speaker's style instead of listening to what the speaker says.	May notice weaknesses in the speaker's style, but pays attention to what they speaker says.
Listens only for major points and ignores details and examples.	Listens for major points and the details that support them.
Gives into daydreaming and becomes distracted.	Resists daydreaming and ignores distractions.
Tunes out when they disagree with the speaker.	Keeps listening even when they disagree with the speaker.
May fall asleep in lectures if tired.	Fights to stay awake if tired.
Does not take good notes.	Takes well-organized notes.

To get more out of lectures, become an active listener. Follow these six steps.

1. Decide to listen—We talked about how deciding to remember is the first step toward increasing your memory's power. Now you must decide to listen. By making this decision, you are strengthening your commitment to learn. Also, by deciding to listen to a lecture, you are taking an active role instead of waiting passively to receive information.

2. Listen with a positive frame of mind—Expect to find something in the lecture that will interest you. As-sume that you will learn something useful, that you will expand your knowledge, and that your understanding of the course will increase.

3. Focus your attention on the speaker—If you

keep your eyes on the speaker, you should be able to ig-nore any distractions that are competing for your attention. Keep your mind on the speaker's topic. Do not give into negative thoughts or feelings about the speaker, the topic, or the speaker's opinions. Your purpose is to learn what the speaker has to say.

4. <u>Encourage the speaker</u>—Look interested. Sit straight but comfortable, and maintain eye contact. Ask ques-tions and make comments when appropriate. Studies of au-dience behavior indicate that a speaker who is getting posi-tive feedback is encouraged to do an even better job. Your posture and expression can communicate to the speaker that you are trying to follow his or her ideas. Everything you do to encourage the speaker also affects you, by mak-ing you concentrate on the lecture.

5. <u>Take notes</u>—Taking notes helps you concentrate on the lecture. Also, taking notes activates another one of your senses (tactile) so that you are more likely to retain the information, especially if you review your notes soon after the lecture. Take notes consistently when listening to lec-tures and adopt or develop a notetaking system that works for you.

6. <u>Decide what is important</u>—Listen for repeated terms or ideas. Speakers use repetition to emphasize important points. Watch for gestures and facial expressions that may also be used for emphasis. Listen for signal words or phrases. A list of signal words and phrases and explanations of what they mean is contained on the following page to as-sist you with this process.

Listening for signal words will help you listen for ideas. For example, if an English instructor says, *"There are four major types of details that may be used to develop a para-graph,"* then you should number from one to four on your paper, skipping lines between them, and listen for the four types of details and the instructor's example of each. If you get to the third type of detail and realize that you don't have anything written down for the second type, then you know you have missed something in the lecture. At this point, you should ask a question.

Signal Words and Phrases

1. **To indicate that another point or example follows:**
also, furthermore, another, moreover, in addition

2. **To add emphasis:**
most important, above all, of primary concern, a key idea, remember that, most significant, pay attention to, the main point

3. **To indicate that an example follows:**
for example, to illustrate, such as, specifically

4. **To indicate a conclusion:**
therefore, in conclusion, finally, to conclude, so, consequently

5. **To indicate an exception to a stated fact:**
however, although, but, though, nevertheless, except

6. **To indicate causes or effects:**
because, due to, consequently, reason, since, cause, result, for, effect

7. **To indicate that categories or divisions will be named or explained:**
types, parts, kinds, characteristics

8. **To indicate a sequence:**
steps, numbers, stages, first, second, etc.

9. **To indicate that items are being compared:**

disavantages, on the other hand, similar, different, equally, in constrast, like

More on Sharpening Your Listening Skills

Good listening is the key to effective notetaking in the classroom.

Do you catch yourself daydreaming during lectures? Do you find gaps in your notes when you read them later? Perhaps you need to sharpen your skills. Researchers believe there are four components to listening. Learning these components will help you sharpen your listening skills, decreasing the gaps in your notes and the internal and external distractions which may occur. The components are:

- *Receiving*: the physiological process of hearing sounds.
- *Attending*: paying attention to a particular set of sounds and ignoring all the surrounding sounds.
- *Comprehending*: understanding what is being said.
- *Remembering*: storing the memory of the message that has been received, attended to, and comprehended.

Here is how you can improve your skills in each of these areas. If you feel you are having difficulty *receiving*, if you are missing every few words that the instructor says or if you are confusing one word for another, move closer to the source of the sound. If this does not help and your classmates do not have the same complaint, you may need your hearing tested.

You can improve your *attending skills* by making a conscious effort to be interested in what is being said. Before a lecture begins, remind yourself that you are there to concentrate and listen. Researchers have found that you can listen up to four times faster than the normal rate of speech. You can put this extra time to good use during a lecture.While you take notes, write down pertinent questions to ask yourself or the instructor. Try to listen for the answers in the lecture.

Your **_comprehending skills_** depend on your language skills and your knowledge of the subject. If you read your textbook and review any specialized terms before a lecture, and if you underline any unfamiliar words in your notes and then actually look them up after a lecture, then your comprehension will increase.

Finally, well-organized notetaking and the consistent use of memory systems, as discussed, will help you *remember* information more clearly. If you are able to recall what you studied in your class notes and what you listened to as the instructor said it, then you will increase your performance on tests.

Use these listening strategies to improve your note-taking:

1. Look at the instructor and pay attention to non-verbal clues; tone of voice, gestures, and body move ments that are meant to relay meaning beyond the spoken words.

2. Picture in your mind's eye what is being said.

Quick Tips to Improve Reading

Reading is an essential skill for all students. The tips contained in this abbreviated section hope to assist you if you have difficulty reading texts or other materials, if you don't really like reading, if you don't understand what you read, if your skills are in need of rejuvenation, if you have been out of school a while, if you can't remember what you have read when it's time to take tests or write papers.

Review and use the strategies on the following page for informational reading:

Purpose	Strategy	When to Use
Reading to understand ideas and construct meaning.	Read carefully at a normal speed, slow down for difficult parts; try to relate ideas.	The first time you read.
Reading to find facts.	Skim/read for dates, names and places. List steps or other factual materials.	Looking for answers pertaining to a test, answers to questions covering chapters, surveying/reviewing chapters or verifying information in you notes.
Reading to analyze difficult or complex passages.	Read slowly. Pay attention to every word. Break sentences apart. Express parts in your own words. Summarize difficult passages.	While reading a sentence or passage that you don't understand; while analyzing difficult sections, reading literature-especially poetry.

Over the next several pages I will attempt to provide some very specific, easy to follow suggestions for improving your academic performance. It is important that you pay close attention to these tips and apply them.

1. Attempt to predict what your reading assignment will cover. You can base this on directions given by the instructor or after you have surveyed the chapter.

2. Always understand your purpose for reading. If unclear on your purpose, ask! It's difficult to proceed if we don't know where we are going right?

3. Attempt to relate what you read to your experiences. Ask yourself does the reading relate in any way to your experiences? If so, great. If not how will it relate to future experiences?

4. Use questions to guide your reading. Remember to

use the chapter headings and make them into questions. Then answer them.

5. Look for patterns of thinking. Are there things repeated?

6. Look for the writer's purpose. Uncover the main idea or topic and you will unmask the purpose.

7. Look for implications in your reading. What is the overall impact of your reading?

8. Define unfamiliar words in context. Look them up and make them part of your vocabulary.

9. Evaluate what you read. Translate it into your own words. *Remember,* the instructor's feedback, your test performance and your increased level of knowledge are all indications of your progress.

Critical thinking is a process of constructing and evaluating meaning. You do this by interpreting what the writer says. A critical thinker uses his/her mind to interpret and understand what others mean, as well as, to attempt to communicate clearly what he/she thinks and why.

The four critical thinking strategies are:

1. Examining assumptions.
2. Make predictions.
3. Sharpen interpretations.
4. Continuous evaluation of what is read.

Constructing guide questions and making predictions about content enable one to read with a purpose, and if there is no purpose, why do it, right?

Remember, there are three main purposes for reading texts or informational material:

1. For information.

2. For facts.

3. For analyzation (of difficult or complex text).

Quick Tips to Improve Writing

Ok, as I am sure you already know, writing is just as vital as reading is to your ultimate success as a student. Writing well requires focused attention, and intense thinking. The ability to express yourself in essays or in other forms of writing will prove key. This abbreviated section will provide specific tips for improving your writing. I will also include tips for applying critical thinking to your writing.

1. Approach writing with a positive attitude.

2. Review the types of writing you have done.Reviewing (your writings) will help you determine what new writing experiences you may need.

3. Review or reflect upon any comments you have received on your writing in the past.

4. Examine whether your papers were evaluated for grammar, content or both. Determine where your strength lies and build from there.

5. Evaluate in which courses you must do extensive writing. What courses are they? Knowing this enables you to plan appropiately.

6. Take a minute to evaluate how you feel about each of the following in terms of your current level of ability and comfort level.

	Hard	Easy
Choosing topic	____	____

Organizing ideas   _____   _____

Thinking of what to say   _____   _____

Writing a thesis/introduction   _____   _____

Coming up with examples   _____   _____

Writing a conclusion   _____   _____

Choosing the right words   _____   _____

Using correct grammar   _____   _____

Spelling correctly   _____   _____

As with anything else, your feelings about everything will dictate your reaction to it. How you feel about writing is controlled by your writing experiences be they good or bad, positive or negative. As a successful student, you must learn to write well. What does writing well mean? It means simply learning to communicate in a clear and effective manner. It means that you are able to communicate your feelings and thoughts easily and convincingly.

Here are some basic characteristics of good writings:

1. They have a purpose. Know yours!
2. They have a controlling idea or thesis.
3. They have a pattern of thought or logical develop ment of an idea. Your writing should flow or con- nect smoothly.
4. The points made are supported in paragraphs.
5. It addresses the appropriate audience for which it is intended.
6. It has specific implication for the reader.
7. The words are selected carefully.

The following tips show the relationships of critical thinking and active writing.

- *Assume*
1. Brainstorm to determine assumptions about a topic and generate ideas.
2. Assume reader is uninformed.

- *Predict*
1. Have a purpose for writing.
2. Plan to guide your thinking; predict the essay topic.

- *Interpret*
1. Explain ideas by stating topics, purpose, and pattern in a thesis.
2. Develop the thesis with points and supporting paragraphs.

- *Evaluate*
1. Write from experience for reliability.
2. Revise for completeness of ideas and for objectivity.
3. Edit for clarity and usefulness.

Keeping a journal is an excellent way to recall what you think or know about a topic. Use it to jot down your thoughts on a variety of issues. Trust me, it will become a treasured resource for essay topics. Here are some additional strategies for your writing:

- **Brainstorming**: As mentioned before, this is done by listing everything you can think of about a topic.
- **Free Writing**: For 5 minutes, write whatever you want about your subject, this allows you to get into your writing without thinking about how difficult it might be.
- **Planning**: Simply make a list of questions about your topics.

• **Drafting**: Write freely at this stage without worries or revisions.

Many students consider *starting* the hardest part of writing. The following suggestions will help you develop a plan for writing which will aid you from beginning to end, as well as guide you in what to include.

The five paragraph plan allows you to focus your attention on developing your ideas. When you must write an essay for an exam, the plan will help direct your thinking and build a context for constructing meaning. This plan is a starting point, it will allow you to gain confidence as a writer.

Let's take a look at the five paragraph plan.

Paragraph 1	Introductions Three part thesis statement	(Introduction)
Paragraph 2	Point and support for first part of thesis	(Body)
Paragraph 3	Point and support for second part of thesis	(Body)
Paragraph 4	Point and support for third part of thesis	(Body)
Paragraph 5	Conclusions Implications	(Conclusion)

This plan is designed to help you through the writing process. It can be expanded as you gain increased confidence with your writing.

As I have said throughout this book, studying and studying effectively is one goal of a successful student. There are numerous strategies available to assist students in developing study systems. These systems cover an array of areas from increasing your math ability to learning foreign languages more efficiently. Here are a few quick tips for developing study systems for diverse subject areas.

Study Systems

You may currently be using systems of this nature. If so, that's great. Continue to refine and expand them to meet your specific styles. If not, try the systems on the following page as a starting point.

Class	What to Study	Try this system
Arithmetic	Sample problems and exercises	Add a practice step for solving problems.
Literature	Elements of fiction, plot, characters, theme, etc.	Expand recite and review to interpret and write.
Foreign Language	Words, meanings, pronunciation, and tenses.	Add flashcards and conjugation charts to your reviewing.
Science	Facts, processes, and principles	Add a draw step to illustrate principles and processes.
Social Sciences	Theories and principles of behavior	Add underlining and marking to the read step. Make charts to compare theories.

Another study system which has been extremely successful in helping students prepare for classes and tests in skill development courses like algebra and foreign languages has been the PREP Study System.

PREP means: **Predict**
Read
Evaluate
Practice

It combines two new steps, predict and evaluate, with the SQ3R system that was discussed earlier. This is how it works!

• **Predict:** Predict or anticipate what your reading assignment will cover. Monitor your understanding as you survey to get an overview and then formulate questions to guide your readings and predict outcomes.

• **Read:** As you read, mark and organize. Carefully read and mark important information. Summarize key ideas or concepts in the margin. (Remember to do this in your own words.) In math, list steps in the margin to jar your memory. To organize information, make notes and study guides. Use lists, note-cards, etc.

• **Evaluate:** Evaluate your progress by connecting new information with what you already know.

• **Practice:** Always, practice, practice, practice. Complete all exercises or problems given, then do some more.

Cramming Tips *(only if you have to)*

Know this first, cramming is <u>unwise</u>. Cramming won't work if you haven't studied at all during the semester. The more courses you have to cram for, the less effective it will be. Cramming is not the same as learning. Without substantial review and practice, material learned in cramming sessions is generally forgotten after one or two days. So why cram? To make the best of the situation, and to get by in a course so that you do better next time. If you've been attentive in class, taken notes and have read or skimmed most of the material, these tips may help you through a tough situation.

1. <u>**Make choices**</u>. Don't try to learn it all when you cram. You can't. Instead pick out a few of the most important elements of the course and learn those backwards, forwards, and upside down. Sometimes these choices will be difficult. You might be tempted to go over everything lightly. Resist this temptation. Chances are, you won't recall a lot of new material during the exam. Be courageous and choose important items. For example, you can devote most of your attention to the topic sentences, tables, and charts in a long reading assignment instead of rereading the whole assignment. A useful guideline is to spend twenty-five percent of cramming time learning new material and seventy-five percent of cramming time drilling yourself on that material.

2. Make a plan. Cramming is always done when time is short. That is all the more reason to take a few minutes to create a plan. Choose what you want to study, determine how much time you have, and set deadlines for yourself.

3. Use mind map review sheets and flashcards. Condense the material you have chosen to learn into mind maps, or flash cards and review repeatedly. Mind maps are diagrams or charts connecting related material.

4. Recite and enunciate. The key to cramming is repetitive recitation. Recitation can burn facts into your brain like no other study method. Go over your material again and again and again. (Remember, say it loud from our earlier chapter.)

5. Relax. You do not learn material well when you cram, you are more likely to freeze and forget it under the pressure of an exam. So relax, use deep breathing and concentrate.

6. Think positively. Consider this approach. Tell yourself it would have been more effective to study earlier and more often. Remind yourself you will have an opportunity to do that next time. Give yourself permission to be only human, but make a committment to prepare properly next time.

Two key things that I will remember and use from this chapter are:_____

_____

7

Just Chill

If there is no struggle, there is no progress.

Frederick Douglass

Conquering Anxieties

Feeling nervous, excited, and anxious? *Remember*, stress is the way your mind and body react to experiences that are new, threatening, or exhilarating. It prepares you to act. The way you respond determines if it will help or hurt. Helpful stress gives you energy. More adrenaline enters the bloodstream, heart and breathing rates increase, blood flow quickens, and muscle strength improves. Harnessing the energy of occasional stress can help you meet physical challenges, solve problems, and reach goals.

Harmful stress comes from a latin word meaning *"to draw tight."* When there's no outlet for this feeling of tightness, this is stress at its worse and it can be quite harmful. Chronic unrelieved stress can cause headaches, backaches, loss of appetite, constant fatigue, depression and other serious physical problems. As a student you want to look for ways to relieve stress that is harmful. As a student, you may experience stress from numerous sources. Identify your sources of stress and make plans to counteract it. The following tips will assist you with coping more effectively with common anxieties.

It's natural for students to feel stress or anxiety about:

Leaving Home—Separating from your family and friends is tough, but it will be much easier if you:
- Keep in touch through letters, phone calls and visits.
- Make new friends by introducing yourself to others or by getting involved in an activity, club or organization.

Commuting to School—Commuters may worry about not having enough personal freedom, to help solve this problem:
- Discuss your concerns with your parents, family and guardians.
- Create a game plan that you both can live with.

Managing Finances—Chances are you'll have to budget your money carefully. Follow these guidelines. Students going away to college will want to pay very close attention; however, these tips are useful for commuting students as well.
- Calculate how much money you will need per semester for such things as tuition, room and board and other standard fees.
- Plan each semester month per month.
- Plan ahead for special expenses, etc.
- Stick to your budget as closely as possible, set priorities.

Sharing with a Roommate—If you will live with a roommate, you should be considerate and show the same respect and consideration that you would like to receive.
- Respect your roommate's space, freedom, opinions, customs and feelings.
- Allow your roommate adequate quiet time and peace. Establish a schedule for study, dating, and other entertainment. Be honest about your likes, dislikes and comfort level.
- Never borrow your roommates belongings without first asking.
- Neatness counts, do your part.
- Discuss problems related to living arrangement as

they arise. Don't sit on concerns or hold them in. This is an important step in growing. Share and be willing to compromise.

Having Values Tested—College is a place to expand and grow in a variety of ways. Expect challenges, awakenings and triumphs. When you meet individuals who have differing opinions and views on subjects such as alcohol, sex, drugs, and religion remember to:
- Listen (try to understand, you may learn something new).
- Hold firm to your beliefs if you feel strongly about an issue.
- Respect the other person's view.

Dealing Effectively with Personal Problems—Conflicts are a natural part of life. It is important to resolve conflicts when they arise, be they with instructors, friends, loved ones, peers, girlfriends or boyfriends. Always attempt to:
- Calm down before discussions.
- Be direct, not angry.
- Seek help if necessary from a counselor, friend or family member.

Real stress is unrelieved anxiety that persists over a long period of time. This can be very harmful if you are not able to manage it. If left unchecked, it can weaken you physically, and impair your ability to reason or think clearly. The warning signs when stress gets out of control are many. Review the list below and see whether you have any of these common symptoms of stress. The more of these you have, the more serious your stress and the more likely it will be that you will need to learn some strategies for coping with stress.

1. Depression or Continuous Sadness
2. Difficulty Falling Asleep
3. Extreme Tiredness and Fatigue

    4. Feelings of Anger or Resentment
    5. Frequent Absence from Work or Classes
    6. Impatience
    7. Inability to Concentrate
    8. Loss of Pleasures in Life
    9. Increase or Decrease in Appetite
  10. Muscular Aches for no Reason
  11. Stomach or Intestinal Disturbances
  12. Sweaty Palms
  13. Tension Headaches
  14. Test Anxiety

Reducing Stress

You've Got to Be Realistic

Change those things which you can. Those things you can't, don't waste your time worrying about them. Unrealistic goals, and believing you must be perfect, will set you up for failure. Your expectations should be reasonable and you should expect to make mistakes. Learn from them.

Exercise Anxiety Away

Move Your Body: Exercise has a natural calming effect. When you feel tense, your muscles tighten. Exercise to relieve this tightness. Practice deep breathing, walking, or aerobics. Whatever you do, just move your body.

Just Say No

You can't be all things to all people! When you are under stress, the last thing you need is more to do. If you have trouble saying no, assertiveness training may help.

Get Help

Sometimes problems may be too much for you to handle alone. Problems seem larger than life when you try going it alone. If you hate to ask for help, get over it, and fast. We all need help from time to time.

Avoid Toxic People

Negative attitudes are deadly; pessimistic outlooks are torture. Negativity will only add to your stress and bring you down even further. If possible, eliminate negative people from your life. This may be difficult, but it is necessary for your well being particularly if you can't counteract their negativity with a positive attitude. Focus on the positive and be realistic.

Get Lost in the Moment

Have some fun. Lose track of time in an activity that makes you forget your worries. Find a hobby where you can relax. Don't worry, be happy.

Love the One You're With

Be good to yourself. Do something nice for yourself especially when you are under stress. You deserve it. Buy yourself a gift, go to a movie, or dinner. Hang out with a friend, one who is positive and enjoys life.

Organize Your Life

Disorganization is a source of stress. Develop a schedule, get your room or house in order. Catch up on what you've missed. Get a physical, see a dentist, make a to-do list and organize your planning. It will work wonders.

Make a Wish-List

Start now to create a wish list of things that you would do if only there was time. When you're dealing with stress, get away and make a wish come true.

Reach Out and Touch Someone

No one can truly help another without helping himself. Helping others makes you feel good and takes your mind off of worrying. Help a friend solve a problem or study for a course. You'll be surprised how much better you'll feel.

Relaxation Exercises

Throughout the remainder of this chapter, I will provide for you some specific exercises which will help you to relax and reduce stress. I have also provided additional tips on successful visualization, affirmations and positive thinking. It is my hope that you will put them to use.

Tension has many negative consequences. Not only does it cause you to feel unpleasant, it also reduces your power of concentration which could lead to mistakes on exams, papers, presentations, at work and on your ability to retain information. Try using relaxation techniques and imagery tips to help you identify and control your physical and mental reactions to stress.

Relaxation exercises will produce a calm, peaceful, relaxed state, while imagery will help you generate pleasant thoughts and allow you to further deepen your relaxation. First learn proper breathing. This will enable you to take in oxygen which purifies your blood and cleanses your body of waste materials. Blood low in oxygen cannot properly nourish tissues and organs. This condition contributes to fatigue, anxiety and depression. Proper breathing is important for you in developing a healthy, mental and physical state.

It is important that you learn the critical elements of proper breathing. When you begin to feel anxious or nervous your breathing becomes shallow, fast, and irregular. This is a signal that you are under stress. At these times you should return your body to a calm, slow, and rhythmic tempo of breathing. To properly breathe deeply requires practice. If while attempting these activities you feel dizzy, light-headed or uncomfortable, stop, relax and try later.

You will soon find yourself able to use your breathing to calm down on-the-spot. Lastly, it is important for you to use the following breathing techniques for the relaxation exercises in this chapter. In this way, you will be able to derive maximum benefit from them.

Exercise A: Calm Abdominal Breathing

Step 1: Get your body into a comfortable and relaxed position. Place your left hand (palm down) over the top of your navel. Now, place your right hand gently on top of your left. Keep your eyes open.

Step 2: Imagine that there is an empty balloon inside your body. It is positioned just below the point at which your hands are placed. Begin to inhale gently. As you take in a breath, imagine that the air is coming in through your nose and filling the balloon.

Notice that your hands begin to rise as this occurs. Continue this pattern as you imagine the oxygen filling the balloon. You will feel your hands rise slightly as you inhale. During your first few practice periods, limit your inhalation to three seconds. With repeated practice, you may choose to extend your inhalation of breaths to four or five seconds.

Step 3: Very slowly, begin to exhale and empty your balloon. And, as you exhale, repeat to yourself—calm, confident, competent. Exhaling will cause your hands to return to their original position. (Adapted from Everly & Rosenfeld, 1981.)

Practice this pattern for two deep breaths followed by five to ten consecutive normal breaths. Then, repeat the pattern. Again, if you feel light-headed, or uncomfortable, stop the exercise. Before beginning any further exercises in this chapter, there are several things you want to do.

- Be sure to remove contact lenses or glasses.
- Loosen your belt and any other articles of tight clothing.
- Find a comfortable, quiet spot.
- Minimize the chance of any disruptions.

Deep Muscle Relaxation

The technique of Progressive Relaxation was described by Dr. Edmund Jacobson in 1929. His method of deep muscle relaxation is based on the notion that muscle tension is the result of the body responding to anxiety-provoking thoughts and situations.

Take just a moment to close your eyes. Imagine that you are sitting in class. The teacher announces that he/she will be calling on students and asking questions about an assigned reading. If you are experiencing anxiety, you will observe that your body is reacting in some way to the thought of the teacher calling on you. Perhaps your shoulders, or your neck muscles contract with tension. If you feel tension in your head, jaws, neck or shoulders, you are experiencing a very common anxiety reaction. The majority of people who complain of tension-related problems, focus their stress in these areas.

In using progressive relaxation, you will be turning your attention to your body and tensing and relaxing muscles. The major groups of muscles in this exercise include:

1. Head, face, throat, and shoulders
2. Hands, forearms, and biceps
3. Chest, stomach, and back
4. Thighs, buttocks, calves, and feet

Exercise B: Progressive Relaxation

Practice this exercise in a comfortable position, holding the tension for three seconds. As you release the tension, try repeating to yourself any of the following sentences:

• I am calm and relaxed.
• My body is calm.
• I am deeply relaxed.
• I am quiet and peaceful.

• The tension is leaving my body.
• I am calm, confident, competent.
• I am serene and strong.

Step 1: <u>Head, Face, Throat and Shoulders</u>

Assume a comfortable position. Wrinkle your forehead as tightly as you can. Hold for three seconds and relax. Feel the difference between a tense forehead and a relaxed one. Repeat the procedure. Next, tense the muscles in your face. Tighten your jaws. Hold the position for three seconds and release. Again, feel the tension fade away. Repeat the tensing. Tense your throat and neck. You can feel the strain on those muscles. Now relax and repeat the tightening. Hunch your shoulders. Try to touch your shoulders to your ears. Hold the position, then let the tension go. Feel the relaxation entering the muscles. Repeat tensing your shoulders.

Step 2: <u>Hands, Forearms and Biceps</u>

Tighten your hands. Make two fists. Experience the tension in your hand. Hold for three seconds and relax. Notice your forearms tightening. Release your hands and allow relaxation to flow into the muscles. Feel the difference relaxation brings. Repeat the procedure. Tense your biceps. Hold the tension and experience the tightness in your arms. Let go of the tension. Feel the relaxation. Repeat this sequence.

Step 3: <u>Chest, Stomach and Back</u>

Focus on your chest muscles. Try to make them very tense. Hold for three seconds. Release and repeat the procedure. Tighten your stomach muscles. Feel the tension in your abdomen. Release and relax. Notice the difference. Now, do it again. Concentrate on the muscles in your back. Tense them and make them tight. Feel the strain on the muscles. Now, allow yourself to go limp. The relaxation spreads across your back. Tighten and relax your back again.

Step 4: <u>Thighs, Buttocks, Calves and Feet</u>

Turn your attention to your thighs. Tighten these muscles. Experience the feeling of tension. Hold for three seconds and relax. Repeat this procedure. Try to tense the muscles of the buttocks. Feel the strain in those muscles. Now relax and let the tension go. Do it again. Using your calves, tense these muscles. Hold the tension in. Release the tightness and feel your legs relax. Again, tighten your calves. Now, relax them. Flex your feet toward your body and hold the tension. Now release. Notice the tension go away. Repeat the procedure.

The progressive relaxation exercise is now complete. You should experience a sense of warmth and relaxation. This feeling is the absence of muscle tension. Should you still feel tightness in any muscle group you need only to repeat that portion of the exercise. Practice this exercise as part of a daily "body check." During the course of the day you will want to check your body for areas which may be responding to anxiety with muscle tension.

Use of Relaxation Exercises

One of the most powerful techniques for learning to relax and achieve a calm state, is the utilization of relaxation exercises. Research has demonstrated that a deepened state of relaxation is associated with increased concentration and recall of information. For you to become a calm, confident and competent student, it is important to master the skill of learning to relax.

You will find that each of these relaxation exercises incorporates the important elements of relaxation: imagery, deep muscle relaxation, proper breathing and positive self-statements. I suggest that you try to practice at least one of these daily. Make sure that you practice in a place where the chances of being disturbed are minimal. If at any time, you have difficulty focusing your attention on the instructions, you may stop and begin again.

Visualizations and affirmations can restructure your attitudes and behaviors. An affirmation is a statement describing what you want. Affirmations are positive reinforcing statements of encouragement. They are most powerful when they are personal, positive, and written in present tense. Many successful people use them effectively. First, decide what you want, and describe yourself as if you already had it. For example, if you decide you want to attend a specific college, you might write: "*I Laura Lynch, have a full scholarship to Harvard University, and enjoy the challenges it presents. My peers and I get along well and my teachers want me to learn.*"

The details in affirmations are what make them work. Use names, involve all your senses. Once you have written one, repeat it. Practice saying it aloud several times a day. Say it regularly, just before bedtime or upon waking.

- Get in a chair and relax.
- Take a few deep breaths.
- Repeat your affirmations with emotion.
- Use a mirror.
- Look at yourself while repeating your affirmations with commitment.

Visualization is the act of seeing yourself as successful.

- Decide what you want to improve.
- Write down what it would:
  - look like,
  - sound like,
  - and feel like to improve it.

If you are planning to lose weight, write down what you would look like, feel like, and wear. Write down how others would react or what they would say. Visualization involves not only sight, but also involves smells, tastes, and textures as well. Once you have a sketch of what it would be like, practice it in your imagination. Rehearse it in your mind. This will improve your ability to focus, take tests or just to relax and enjoy private time.

Here are some affirmations to practice. Remember you can also personalize them by creating your own. I _____ am healthy, have great energy all day, exercise often, eat wisely, have great grades, plan my time wisely, learn quickly, work hard, am wealthy, like myself, am positive and helpful.

Two key things that I will remember and use from this chapter are:_____

8

Working Your Plan

One's work may be finished someday, but one's education, never.

Alexandre Dumas

Test Preparation, Types, Approaches

As you know, tomorrow belongs to those who prepare for it today. Preparation is a major component to your success. Never stop believing in yourself, not for a moment. Don't give into the negativity. Map out the road on which you wish to travel. It's all in your hands. Prepare and go on strong and determined, a winner.

Most students, if not all students, experience nervousness on test day. If you prepare adequately you will markedly decrease your level of test anxiety. It will decrease your fears of feeling you're underprepared. It will also help you decrease one of the biggest fears of students, "not being able to remember the material you studied."

Tests, as you know, are a necessary gauge of your progress, and of course they show a degree of what you have learned. Objective and subjective tests are the two basic types. Effective study methods and sufficient preparation will improve your chances for academic success. Let's get started. Here are ten tips on how to study for tests.

1. Always allow sufficient time for study, cramming usually doesn't work and adds to your level of stress.
2. Organize your material, and know what to study.
3. Create a study method, use the SQ3R, or prep systems we discussed or create your own system.
4. Review past exams, notes and assignments. They provide excellent hints for test preparation.
5. Review the errors you've made in the past. Do you know what they are? This is the time to correct them.
6. Practice relaxation exercises before, during, and after exams. This will help you remain calm during testing, be less distracted in class and unwind afterwards.
7. If you enter a test situation feeling mentally and physically prepared you're doing something right. Keep it up.
8. Develop and use a test preparation and test taking routine and follow it consistently.
9. Practice samples of multiple choice, true/false and fill in the blank tests. Practice makes perfect or at least helps you ease tension and gain familiarity.
10. Learn how to plan and write an essay exam.

How you feel will affect how you perform on a test; therefore, expecting to do well will increase your chances for success. Self-confidence will aid in directing your energy toward success. The best advice I can give you for preparing for examinations is simply to stress being prepared. Be prepared for the type of exam being given; be ready for all possible questions. Master your subjects thoroughly and organize as well.

To help you prepare for every test and to ease the inevitable tension that arises follow these essential steps.

1. Create a study calendar/schedule.
2. Decide what to study.
3. Use a study system.

Doing these things will enable you to answer three extremely important questions: When should you study? What should you study? How should you study?

Create a Study Calendar

Creating a study calendar or schedule, will allow you to have greater control of your study time; not only that, it will establish fixed times for you to review. In time these reviews will become second nature, a good habit. For this to be effective, allow time in your schedule for daily, weekly, and exam reviews.

How to Organize Your Reviews

Plan daily reviews; take five to fifteen minutes a day for each of your classes. Review your notes and assignments for the previous class. Do this as soon as possible after your class. Review new material relating it to what you have already learned. This will help make those vitally important connections among topics and will provide you with an opportunity to gain a greater perspective of the course(s). Keep in mind the standard study rule; two hours for every one spent in class.

Each week take an hour to an hour and a half to review each of your courses. This is extra time you may spend beyond doing assignments. During this time, review all of your notes and study guides. Always attempt to anticipate test questions based on what has been discussed in class or in readings. This is an in-depth look at what you covered in your course(s) for the week. Always relate current work to previous work. Determine how the new material fits.

Tests/Exam Reviews

Begin your test review at least one week before your scheduled exam. Make this a major review which should be far more involved than your weekly review because it could cover several weeks of material. Prepare by reviewing lecture notes, text notes, study guides, notecards, all handouts, previous tests, papers or graded assignments. Because you have done daily and weekly reviews, the material will be familiar. At this point continue to anticipate and answer test questions. Exam reviews may take anywhere from two to two and a half hours.

While conducting research for this book, it was consistently discovered that the test/exam reviews have caused the greatest difficulty for students. They take longer to do, they cover a large amount of material and are the hardest for students to commit to doing regularly; however, I can't stress enough that they are also vital to your success.

The following are four key tips taken from earlier chapters worthy of repeating. Use them! Try these suggestions for increasing your concentration for these longer study sessions. They tend to work when you are attempting to study for two or more hours in length.

Tip #1: Schedule your review at the time of day when you are most alert. Are you a morning person? Are you a night person? This is important self-knowledge you should know.

Tip #2: Study for your hardest exam first. This will require the greatest output of energy; so do it first.

Tip #3: Take a break every hour. Get up and walk around, grab a snack. Do something unrelated to studying.

Tip #4: Reward yourself for getting the job done. Make plans to go to a movie, to visit friends, or to just do something fun when you have finished reviewing your exam.

How to Decide What to Study for Tests/Exams

The sources of the questions on your test will be derived from a multiplicity of areas. We reviewed many of them earlier—notes, chapters, textnotes, study guides, previous tests, papers, homework, and other graded assignments. It is probably not necessary to review material you already know; however, a brief review wouldn't hurt.

Review your lecture notes, they will provide wonderful supplemental information. Within your text, review your underlining and marginal notes. Look closely at your additional notes, outlines, notecards, and other study materials. As I shared earlier, your previous test are vital resources. They allow you insight into the types of questions which might arise. You can also review any past errors for the sake of correcting them.

The task of reviewing handouts provided by your instructor is another necessary step. Another strategy for helping you prepare for tests is to set up a time for group study. Studying with others is an excellent way to gain greater perspective. Remember, two heads are better than one, at least most times.

How You Should Study Through the Use of Study Systems

It's a well-known fact that once you decide what to study, how you study will determine the effectiveness of your review. Use a study system. Review the systems we discussed earlier, the SQ3R and PREP or as I said before adopt a system of your own. Here is an example of what you might do to prepare for a big exam in one of your classes.

Sample Plan

A. Approximately one week prior to your scheduled exam, take two or more hours to review *all* chapters and topics that the test might cover. Take a break after about one hour to keep from tiring and losing concentration. Plan to study specific material in several short sessions.

Organize It

B. Your materials should be organized by type: lecture notes, textnotes, study guides, handouts, past assignments and tests. Organize them by chapter or topic. Keep a list of concerns or specific questions or information you believe will appear on the test.

C. If you review facts, terms, formulas, steps in a process, or something similar, try using 3 x 5 notecards and carry them in your pocket, purse, book bag or daytimer. Take them wherever you go. You'd be surprised how much you might learn while waiting for a bus. Use the cards for recitation either silently or aloud. Remember when you do it aloud you incorporate an additional sense, which increases retention.

D. Map or diagram items you believe might be harder to remember. When studying, try drawing them from memory. While taking an exam, close your eyes and try to visualize your illustrations.

E. Each day prior to the actual test, review your maps and other illustrations. Go over them again the night before your test, before going to sleep. Believe it or not, research has shown that studying before sleeping improved retention. Review one last time the day of the test.

Try these strategies to help you create a test routine. They will help you stay relaxed, and also help you avoid distractions. Utilize these steps on test day:

#1-Be prompt; sit near the front of the class in order to be less distracted. Close your eyes. Take a few breaths and think like a winner.

#2-Write down memory cues. As soon as you arrive, write on your test any cues which may help trigger your memory. This will help boost your confidence.

#3-Skim or survey your test as soon as you receive it. Skim to see how long it is, what type of test it is, and the point system. This will also help you plan your time.

#4-Always read the directions carefully (to avoid needless mistakes).

#5-After skimming, attack easy questions first.

#6-Planning your time eliminates rushing. Spend most of your time working with test items yielding the highest points. Always read an exam in its entirety prior to turning it in.

#7-Don't waste too much time pondering perceived difficult items. Skip them and return later.

#8-Guessing is all right (if there is no penalty). Don't leave any questions blank if at all possible.

#9-Stay focused. Focus on the test, relax, stay positive. (Talk positively to yourself.) Remember, positive self-talk works. Just say *"I'm prepared; I'm relaxed; I'll pass."*

#10-Re-read final exam copy. Proofread for careless errors. First choices are usually correct, so don't change answers unless you're sure.

#11-Learn from past performance. Each paper is a resource, use it to learn from your mistakes.

It is a necessary skill for successful students to learn to "disarm" tests. Disarming a test is merely taking the mystery or fear from it. You do this by preparing appropriately, asking your instructor what to expect, using memory aids, and any of the strategies we previously discussed. Note the following winning test taking tips.

Your instructor may choose to give any variety of test types, become familiar with each of the following.

Multiple Choice

- Check directions. See if more than one answer is acceptable.
- Answer in your head first before looking for possible answers.

- Check off questions you can't answer. Return later to complete.
- Read all answers before choosing.
- If two answers are indeed similar, except for one or two words, choose one of those answers.
- If two answers have similar sounding or looking words, choose one of those answers.
- If answers call for a sentence completion, eliminate the answers that are not a grammatical fit for the sentence.
- Eliminate answers you know are incorrect first.
- All of the above or none of the above responses are usually right.
- If two quantities are almost the same, select one.
- If answers cover a wide range, choose one in the middle.

True/False

- Read and select your answers.
- One word can make the statement wrong. If any part is false, all of it is false.
- Look for qualifiers like all, most, sometimes, never, or rarely. These are key words. Absolute qualifiers such as always or never generally mean it's false.
- Mark it true unless you know for sure it's false. These types of exams usually have more true answers than false ones.

Machine Graded, Scannable Tests

- Watch for stray marks, they can look like answers.
- Make sure your answer corresponds to the questions you are answering.
- Check your test booklet against the answer sheet when you switch sections and begin at the top of each column.

Open Book Test (These are harder than they sound.)

- When studying for your exams, review your texts thoroughly.

- Write down any formulas you will need on a piece of paper, use paper clips or bookmarks to hold pages, this will save time looking through pages. Number your notes.

Short Answers/Fill-in-the-Blank Questions

- These questions often require definitions or descriptions.
- Concentrate on key words and facts (keep it brief).
- Over learning pays off here.

Essay Questions

- Be precise.
- Make an outline first.
- Get to the point.
- Include part of the question in your answer.
- Usually require either a short answer or a developed one of length.
- Read carefully and understand.
- Follow instructions.
- Stay on topic, focus.
- Always write legibly.
- Use an appropriate writing instrument.

Key Words to Look for When Doing Essay Questions

- Analyze (break it apart)
- Compare (examine two or more things)
- Contrast (show differences)
- Criticize (make judgements)
- Define (give the meaning)
- Describe (give details)
- Discuss (consider and debate)
- Enumerate (list several ideas)
- Explain (make an idea clear)
- Evaluate (give your opinion)
- Illustrate (give concrete examples)

- Outline (describe main ideas, characteristics, events)
- Prove (support with facts)
- Relate (show the connections)
- State (explain precisely)
- Summarize (give a brief account)

Nine Key Strategies for Increasing Your Standardized Test Scores

1. Know how many sections are on the test and what each section will cover. Inquire as to whether essays are re-quired.

2. Find out if it will be timed, how long will it last and how much time for each section. If the test is longer than two hours, take a snack for an energy boost.

3. If an essay is necessary, practice timed essays. This is great practice.

4. Find out what test aids will be allowed—dictionary, calculator, etc.

5. Purchase pencils and exam books if necessary.

6. Get a good night's sleep; eat a nourishing breakfast; arrive on time, think positively.

7. Use guessing strategies.

8. During breaks, stretch and move around; it will help you to become more alert.

9. Check over your answers; erase stray marks and do not leave any questions blank.

Special Techniques for Math and Science Tests

1. *Translate problems into English*. Putting problems into words aids your understanding. When you study equations and formulas, put those into words, too. The words help you see a variety of applications for each formula. For example, *the Pythagorean Theorem*, $4 = 2 + 2$, $(C = A + B)$ can be translated as *"The square of the hypotenuse of a right triangle is equal to the sum of the squares of the other two sides."*

2. *Perform opposite operations*. If a problem involves multiplication, check your work by dividing; if it involves adding, then subtract; factoring, then multiply; taking the square root, then square differentiating the intergate.

3. *Use time drills*. Practice working problems quickly. Time yourself. Exchange problems with a friend and time each other. You can also do this in a study group.

4. *Analyze before you compute*. When a problem is worth a lot of points, read it twice, slowly. Take time to analyze a problem because you may see ways to take computational short-cuts.

5. *Make a picture*. Draw a picture or a diagram if you are stuck. Sometimes a visual representation will clear a blocked mind.

6. *Estimate first*. Estimation is a good way to double-check your work. Doing this first can help you notice if your computations go awry, and then you can correct the error quickly.

7. *Check your work systematically*. When you check your work, ask yourself: Did I read the problem correctly? Did I use the correct formula or equation? Is my arithmetic correct? Is my answer in the proper form? Avoid the temptation to change an answer in the last few minutes unless you're sure the answer is wrong. By rushing to finish the test in a last minute, it's easier to choose the wrong answer.

8. *Review formulas*. Right before the test, review any formulas you'll need to use. Then write them out on scratch paper as soon as possible during the test.

Keep and review these basic survival techniques. Working with each of these together will help you with academic success.

1. Content Review Skills

Remember to:
• Review assigned readings.
• Review classnotes and reading notes.
• Test yourself.
• Use management techniques.
• Form a study group.
• Use self-monitoring to determine test readiness.

2. Test Management Skills

Remember to:
• Record test dates.
• Plan time for test preparation.
• Avoid cramming.
• Plan to arrive early.
• Keep track of time during the test.

3. Test Wiseness Skills

Remember to:
• Determine what the test will cover.
• Determine the question format.
• Understand the importance of the test.

• Bring items needed for the test.
• Sit in a good location.
• Read test directions carefully.
• Answer easy questions first.
• Use appropiate techniques for answering test questions.

4. Psychological Coping Skills

Remember to:
• Use relaxation techniques.
• Use positive thinking.
• Recognize and express feelings of anxiety.
• Overlearn material.

Overcoming Test Anxiety

Test anxiety surfaces in a variety of forms such as headaches, stomach aches, sweating, forgetfulness, nervousness and more. This section will attempt to provide you with some additional tips to overcome dreaded test stress. Let's first examine if you suffer from test anxiety and if so, at what level?

Here are some real signs of test anxiety. Take a minute, review them and see where you fit. At test time do you:

	Yes	No
1. Have trouble sleeping the night before?	___	___
2. Have sweaty palms?	___	___
3. Get headaches?	___	___
4. Become nauseated and have to leave?	___	___
5. Panic or don't show for class?	___	___
6. Have pains in your back, neck, or legs?	___	___
7. Feel your heart pounding before or during?	___	___
8. Feel nervous and jittery?	___	___
9. Have tightness in you chest or have trouble remembering?	___	___
10. Lose your appetite?	___	___

11. Make careless errors   ____ ____
12. Experience your mind going blank?   ____ ____
13. Worry when others finish first?   ____ ____
14. Feel pressed for time?   ____ ____
15. Worry about your performance and
    believe everyone else is doing great?   ____ ____
16. Think about tests you've failed?   ____ ____
17. Feel like your studying was a flop?   ____ ____
18. Feel like you're not thinking clearly?   ____ ____
19. Have a hard time understanding or
    remembering directions?   ____ ____
20. After taking your test, do you suddenly
    and vividly remember the answers you
    couldn't remember during the test?   ____ ____

If you answered yes to the majority of the questions above, you do suffer from test anxiety at both the physical and psychological levels.

Test anxiety is a learned reaction that can be unlearned. I will attempt to give you a better understanding of it as well as provide some proven strategies for coping and reducing this type of anxiety. It is quite normal to experience some form of test anxiety from time to time. Anxiety is only a severe problem when it defeats us.

What Is Test Anxiety and Its Causes

The reasons vary for test anxiety. Students have expressed the following reasons most frequently as the root of their anxiety: feelings of not living up to the expectations of others and the feeling that they might be rejected in some way if they do not succeed.

People who love you only want the best for you. They want you to succeed. They also will understand if sometimes you fall short of your mark. In setting your goals and expectations, make sure that they are what you want. If you prepare yourself, do your very best, and still fall short of your mark—you tried. Pick yourself up, dust yourself off, learn from your mistakes and move on. After all life is all about learning. Students many times feel that grades are an estimation of their personal worth.

Grades are just a part of the person you are. Your personal worth is far too valuable to be measured by a test grade. Grades simply measure the degree to which you have learned a particular subject. Many students place an exorbitant emphasis on scores. One score will not make or break you. If you feel you could do better, *just do it* the next time around. Many students give in to feelings of guilt during the test because they didn't prepare.

If this is you, then focus. Yes, you should have reviewed for your test. Your score would probably be better if you had. However, this is the moment of truth. Concentrate and do the very best you can. The next time put the effort into preparing. Believe it or not many students feel truly helpless when it comes to exams. They feel that they have absolutely no control over their performance or grades.

As a successful student, you have much of the control. By taking control and doing all the things necessary to prepare and review you will achieve success.

The beliefs and perceptions many students have about their parent's and others' expectations are many times inaccurate. Give them credit for loving and supporting you through it all. Grades should never translate into statements of worth, *"I'm no good," or "I'm dumb,"* etc. This only destroys your self-esteem and creates more anxiety.

More Tips on Relaxing and Staying Calm

A sure fire way to beat test anxiety is simply to calm down, chill, don't go there, relax. ***Relaxation*** reduces the physical and mental uneasiness brought on by test anxiety. It is a well-known fact that you cannot be relaxed and anxious at the same time. Once you learn how to relax, you will be able to focus your attention on doing well on your test.

Muscle relaxation exercises as discussed earlier are a

good way to control the physical symptoms of test stress. Try this:

A. Close your eyes.
B. Search for tension in your body;
    1. clenched teeth
    2. hunched shoulders
    3. crossed legs
C. Breathe deeply.
D. Sit comfortably.
E. Release tension.
    1. Clench your hand into a fist.
    2. Squeeze your fist tightly.
    3. Hold for a few seconds and release slowly.

When you are experiencing test anxiety, your mind is very similar to a clenched fist; when you relax it transforms into an open hand, releasing tension.

Try the following exercises for relaxing in the classroom. They're fun and easy. The best part about them is that no one will even know you're doing them.

A. Breathe deeply, drop your shoulders. Place your hands in your lap and clench your fists to relieve *real* tension. Slowly open your hands and let them drop down to your sides. Let go of *all* tension.

B. Place your elbows on your desk, bow your head while resting your forehead on top of your hands. You can either close your eyes or leave them open. The key is to focus on breathing slowly and deeply until you feel calm.

Distractions are a major cause of anxiety during testing. *Try* focusing on the test.

• While papers are being passed out, silently review what you have studied.

• When you get your test, read each question. Look only at the test.

If you need to relax or to think over an answer, close

your eyes so that you won't notice what is going on around you.

Don't focus on other students. *Also, avoid* <u>self-pre-oc-cupation</u>. Don't focus on any physical discomfort unless it's so severe that you wouldn't be able to test. Don't focus on the likelihood that you might fail. Trust me, these thoughts will steal your attention. Fight distracting thoughts. Simply concentrate and:

- Re-read if you need to.
- Review mentally what you have studied that is related to the test.
- Underline or circle key words.
- Read slowly, whisper or move lips to involve your other senses.

In an earlier chapter we talked about positive self-talk. This is an important weapon against anxiety. You must learn to listen to yourself and correct any negative messages you're sending. Negative thinking is a habit for many. As you know, it takes work to break a habit, especially a bad one. Try these tips to break the habit and to maintain a successful attitude.

1. Start to listen to the messages you are sending your-self, especially if they are negative. *"I'm going to fail"; "I hate my class"; "My instructor doesn't care."*

2. Instantly replace negative thoughts with positive ones such as, *"I will pass"; "I'm learning in this class"; "The instructor wants me to achieve."*

3. Change your inner voice, (that voice inside your head) to a calm and confident one.

Try this:

<u>*Meditation Exercise*</u>—To practice the kind of positive thinking that can make you a more successful student, fol-low these steps.

1. Select a time of day or night when you are alone and won't be disturbed.
2. Find a quiet, comfortable place such as your bed room. Go in and close the door.
3. Lie flat on the floor, on your back.
4. Put a pillow under you head if you need one.
5. Place your arms down at your sides with your palms open and leave the backs of your hands resting on the floor.
6. Breathe slowly and deeply through your nostrils; ex hale through your mouth.
7. Release any tension that you feel in your body.
8. Concentrate on becoming calm and relaxed. Empty your mind of all other thoughts.
9. When you feel completely calm, speak positively to yourself with your inner voice. Say the words that you alone know will make you feel confident and capable of doing your best.
10. Open your eyes. Remain lying down for a few minutes to enjoy feeling confident and calm. Then get up and resume your day's or night's activities.

Use some or all of these coping strategies to help with test anxiety. This is only a partial list. Please feel free to add any others that have worked for you, and by all means, pass them on.

Tip #1: Prepare and prepare well. Calm down by using relaxation techniques.

Tip #2: Listen to your body. Learn its signals for stress.

Tip #3: Dress comfortably. Do not wear tight clothes. Be aware of the room temperature and be prepared for changes.

Tip #4: Wear your favorite fragrance or cologne. Many students are able to relax by smelling familiar and pleasant fragrances.

Tip #5: Be prompt, but not too early. Arriving too early and having to wait may cause great tension or shake your confidence. Listening to other students talk may create undue stress. In terms of tardiness, don't even try it! Winners prepare and expect to win. Tardiness is not an option. Be there on time.

Tip #6: Create a test day tradition:

   • Carry a special pen.

   • Wear your lucky socks.

   • Listen to a special song.

Remember, nothing takes the place of preparation; however, this type of thing is fun and works to build confidence. When dealing with negative thoughts and test anxiety, these additional suggestions have been provided for your use and achievement.

Special Advice for Staying On Top

Dealing with the negative thoughts during review or testing

1. Yell "Stop!" (if you can); whispering works too!
2. Take a moment to daydream (pleasant thoughts only).
3. Visualize success (sound familiar).
4. Focus (it works).
5. Praise yourself (I can do this).
6. Consider the worst and then snap back into reality.

Dealing with negative feelings during review or testing

1. Breath deeply (take two minutes to breath in the positive energy).
2. Search your body for tension (find it and relieve it).
3. Tense and relax (we tried this earlier. Keep it up).
4. Use guided imagery (create your ideal world. Take a mind trip. Just don't forget to return).
5. Describe it (what are you feeling, and why).

7. If all else fails, get help! Depression and anxiety are common among students. If it becomes too much for you, especially after a day or two, please talk to some one; your counselor, parents or a doctor. Don't ignore this, please.

Use these special techniques to deal with anxiety brought on by tests. By carefully applying the suggestions noted in this section, test anxiety can be effectively dealt with over time. The bottom line is to prepare yourself and expect to win.

Two key things that I will remember and use from this chapter are:_____

_____

9

Networks that Work

Success doesn't come to you . . . you go to it.

Marva Collins

Building a Support Network

Everyone needs support from time to time. It is foolish to believe that we don't need help from others. Identify those around you who can be relied upon for consistent and positive support. As a successful student it will be very important that you form support systems both in and out of class.

Within the classroom you should attempt to make friends with individuals who not only have similar approaches and views as you, but individuals who may have differing views or cultures. This will allow you to grow on several different levels through exposure. Forming a study group is an exciting way to meet new friends. Many students join various student clubs as a means of finding support. Research has indicated that students who are involved in extra-curricular activities tend to perform better academically. It is my belief that these students also tend to be self-motivated.

Utilize all of the resources at your disposal. Resources consists of people, organizations, services, publications and activities. The people around you are the most vital resources. Establishing good relationships will help you immensely.

Many students never adequately use the resources available to them. These resources are in place to help you become and remain successful. Investigate resources like student organizations which are great sources of fun, friends and intellectual development.

Making Successful Choices

Throughout your life, you will be required to make choices. It is in your best interest to always make the best and wisest choices possible, considering all options and outcomes. If you use the resources available to you when making decisions, choices about classes, majors, and careers you will experience far less anxiety and stress.

Academic Advisors—can help you better select courses based on your interest and goals. Remember, your advisor will be a guide for you as you work through your general education requirements, as well as your selected major. Developing a schedule that is manageable is very important. Let your advisor know if you have:

1. Specific family obligations, i.e., daycare pickup.
2. Part-time job.
3. Extra-curricular activities.

Counselors—counselors are a wealth of information. Visiting a counselor can be helpful in laying the ground-work for your academic experience. Many students avoid the counseling center because of an imaginary stigma which makes them feel that only students *"with problems"* go there. Don't be fooled and miss out on valuable information and guidance. Counselors can help you:

1. decide on a major
2. with interpersonal relationships
3. with tips on studying

4. work through a crisis
5. identify strengths and areas to improve your abilities
6. find college and community resources
7. when you need someone to listen and much more

Career Counselors—can provide information about your process goals.

1. Visit the career development office and review materials and services provided.
2. Take a vocational preference test to measure your interests and strengths.

Visit a counseling or career center to utilize vocational software to help you with your decision making. Discover, Sigi Plus and Visions are three software packages used to help solidify choices.

The counseling center, as I mentioned earlier is an excellent place to find a listening ear. They can guide you to other sources of assistance as well. Creating a supportive environment is an important asset. If you are able to create the right kind of atmosphere for yourself in school and at home, it will really enrich your life. The need to be a part of a group, to feel needed, and to belong is a basic human need.

The environment provided at school, gives you a perfect opportunity to make new friends, learn new things, and broaden your overall experiences. It is advisable that you begin now to develop a supportive social network. This network should consist of individuals you trust and on whom you can depend. Relationships of this nature are critical. The assistance provided by these relationships is invaluable.

Research has indicated that an individual's vulnerability to psychological and physical problems increase as the number of people providing support decreases. Take time to reach out and connect with others. Many students feel alone and have many fears about the future. These fears can be diminished if connections with others are sought. Make an effort to talk to others and initiate conversations. Through casual conversations, you can find out what others may have in common with you and build on it.

This may be a little scary at first, if you are used to being a loner, but trust me it will be worth the effort in the long run. You will learn that others indeed share your interests, concerns and wishes. Getting involved in special activities, as discussed earlier, is a great way to gain excellent information, and potential growth experiences.

Activities like the student union, special clubs, fraternities, sororities and athletics, provide a wonderful chance to meet individuals who can help to enrich your life and you, theirs. I realize I mentioned the role the counseling center plays in a student's overall development and guidance throughout school; however, I feel the need to reiterate its role and importance and also attempt to cancel out any fears or hesitations you might have in pursuing its use.

It is proven that any difficulties left unresolved may spill over into your academic life. These difficulties may make it very difficult to concentrate; they may surface as a lack of enthusiasm and interest in your day to day functioning—difficulty in sleeping, depression and other negative responses. Counseling centers contain a vast amount of information. If you have any of these concerns, please talk to someone. Being a student can be stressful and going to see a counselor doesn't mean you're nuts. It means you're smart enough to seek the assistance needed to help with your academic and personal success. The counseling center is available to get you through difficult times. So as you can see, there is a lot to be gained and learned in your counseling center, so check it out.

Special Tips for Staying on Top

- •Use your catalog and syllabus. Understand the expectations that your instructors have.
- •Seek out your advisor to get answers to your questions.
- • Get involved in a study group.

- Learn the academic system, how, and when to add/drop classes.
- Learn how and when to register. Learn relevant poli cies and procedures.
- Use the services and resources available in school and in your community.
- Focus, prepare and execute. Always focus on your objectives; plan a process for achieving and execute the plan.
- Understand that stress is natural, yet if it is prolonged and or prevents your functioning get help!
- Be realistic.
- Have fun! After all, this is the best part.

Two key things that I will remember and use from this chapter are:_____

_____

10

Advice for African-American Scholars

Intellectuals ought to study the past, not for the pleasure they find in doing so, but to derive lessons from it.

Cheih Anta Diop

L earn from the past. There are valuable lessons that must be learned from those who proceed us. "The path is clear, the reward tremendous. Those who don't learn from history are bound to repeat it." Learn from the worst of it, thrill in the best of it. The information in this section was written with the African-American scholar in mind; however, all scholars might find it equally as useful. As an African-American scholar, I have found the following insights invaluable.

Building on the Legacy

As an African-American scholar, you will no doubt be confronted with some unique challenges. I strongly urge you to view them as just that, challenges. It has been confirmed that as a people, we are conquerors, we are survivors. Use your history to inspire you.

There are still some who may believe that the color of your skin has some bearing on your overall ability. Don't believe it. Our history is one of great triumph, full of wonderful lessons and brilliant role models; it's full of people overcoming, surviving, and achieving despite adversity.

There are some who question and have low expectations of the African-American scholar's academic motivation and potential. The lessons of the past and of our accomplishments both then and now are a direct contradiction to this belief. Don't fall prey to foolish assumptions, myths or half truths about who we are as a people or who you are as an individual.

As a scholar in general, and as an African-American scholar in particular, I urge you to increase your self-confidence. This, I know, is sometimes not easy; however, I need you to believe in the beauty of your possibilities. Believe in the things that you can accomplis;, hold on to this belief when others may not support you. Prepare your mind, as I have stated numerous times throughout this book. Preparation pays, as will consistency and perserverance.

You are an important part of the history of your people. It is a proud, strong, intelligent and noble heritage. There is an old adage that nothing in life is free. With this thought in mind, I challenge you to put in the necessary time, effort and hardwork to win and achieve your goals.

I wish for you a thirst for true knowledge and insight. Many students feel a sense of powerlessness or lack of control in their lives. Don't let this throw you completely off balance. Developing and implementing effective support and coping systems is a must in helping you gain greater control. If you are to truly survive and thrive, recognize that you can't control everything, but those things that you can control, do so and focus on the outcomes you desire.

Tips to Excel

As an African-American scholar, I offer these tips to help you continue your journey of excellence.

Remember:
1. Don't attempt to be someone you're not. Listen to your *own* heart and follow your dreams.

2. Get in touch with that special part of you that will inspire not only yourself, but others.
3. Surround yourself with positive images, positive people, and positive messages.
4. Don't allow others to bring you down; do learn from constructive criticism, and move on.
5. Never be ashamed of where you come from; you are the sum total of all your experiences. They have helped make you who you are today. Appreciate that.
6. Build your confidence; it will be key to your success.
7. If you need help, get help.
8. Help someone else.
9. Don't be afraid to make a mistake. Mistakes breed wisdom.
10. Have fun.
11. Want more than just to exist.
12. Value family and the role you play.
13. Your word *must* mean something.
14. Let others be able to count on you.
15. Be clear on your values and what is important to you.
16. Ultimately, what you look like and what you wear will not be as important as what you know and how you treat people.
17. Accept yourself. Learn to love who you are.
18. Take time to know yourself. Learn your history; build on it, and let it propel you forward.
19. Recognize that you are special and that everything about you is a reason for celebration.
20. Don't believe the hype. There are those who expect you to fail and believe that you are not capable. You can achieve anyway!
21. Believe in someone or something greater than yourself. This will provide great comfort during difficult times and greater joy during happy times.
22. Use your history to spur you to greater heights.
23. Take the good from all that is around you.
24. Take care of your mind, body and spirit.
25. Seek wisdom.
26. Be kind.

27. Don't take yourself to seriously.
28. Be the best that you can be.
29. Don't make excuses.
30. Expect excellence.
31. Seek truth.
32. Strive to achieve inspite of your circumstances.
33. Respect yourself and your dreams.
34. If you fall down, get up. Struggles build character.
35. Read, it will expand all that you are.
36. Hold your head up, be proud.
37. Expect to be challenged.
38. Rise to the challenge.

Many of the following academic suggestions and strategies are contained throughout the book. However, I believe that they are so important that they were worth emphasizing and repeating. This is vital information to a student's success.

1. Get organized.
2. Dedicate yourself to studying.
3. Prepare yourself and followup.
4. Develop a routine for academic preparation and stick with it.
5. Study with friends. Get involved with culturally diverse groups. Expose yourself to opportunities to learn from others who may use different approaches.
6. Get involved in class.
7. Don't shy away from questions. It's okay.
8. Review your notes daily; use them to prepare for the next class session, and to provide a source of possible questions.
9. Show up. You can't get it if you're not there.
10. Set realistic objectives and go for it.
11. Set priorities.
12. Let the instructors know about your interests and concerns.
13. Desire to succeed.

14. Believe that you are capable.

15. Teach others.

16. When deciding on a career path or other life choice, choose those things that you are passionate about. That passion will ignite your success.

Having earned degrees from an historically Black institution and from a predominantly White institution, the tips here represent a compilation of ideals which helped me survive and excel in both environments. They are offered to you as food for thought. The perspective one takes of a situation determines how one reacts to it. Attempting to view situations as opportunities to learn or as challenges to be overcome, has been a very effective approach for me.

I encourage you to never underestimate your capabilities. When possible, seek out a person who represents the best of what you would like to become. One who will make the time to assist you, one you can trust and whom will offer you unconditional support and guidance.

African-American scholars, it is vital to learn what motivates and inspires you. In knowing this, you find a source of strength. We must find that light which propells us to soar like the phoenix despite our circumstances or perceived limitations. It is my belief that a solid education still remains a clear solution to many of the concerns that we currently face and it is a necessary ingredient to our success. However, it is not the only ingredient in our recipe for excellence as a person. Who we are inside, our relationship with ourselves and others are also key ingredients in this formula. These components combined will equal what I consider a true measure of success and excellence.

I am often asked, what has inspired me, as an African-American scholar, propelling me to achieve. In my quest to discover those inspirations and reasons for my desire to excel and to be the best person I can, I discovered a key source of my strength.

I am inspired and motivated by my mother, who is the wisest and most generous person I have ever met. Instilling in me a sense of determination and spirituality that has sustained me over the years. Upon meeting challenges, it was she who encouraged me to see them as opportunities, as I now encourage you. Regardless of the situation, she never lost faith, gave up hope or stopped believing in herself, insisting that I do the same.

I stand amazed as I reflect on the pure joy she receives from helping and encouraging others. At seventy-six years of age, she still possesses the same courage, determination, and belief in the power of hard work and education. It is this type of commitment and faith that I wish for you. I know that you can achieve all that you desire if you prepare, plan and execute. Start now, believe and succeed.

11

Practical Tips for Instructors of Diverse Populations

C lassrooms are changing, specfically the composi-
tions of our classes are changing. As they change the
needs and approaches utilized in instruction must also change.
Having instructed in the public school system, and at the
college level, I can attest to these rapidly changing environments. As instructors of diverse populations which will over
time grow more multicultural, what lessons can be learned?
Well, there are many lessons.

First Lesson: The world of education is constantly changing.
Second Lesson: It must change to respond to a society that
is becoming more culturally diverse.

Our country will continue to diversify. Minorities now
make up 21.3 percent of the nation's population. With higher
birth rates and increasing numbers of immigrants from Cen-
tral and South America, Asia, and Africa, minorities will continue to make up a larger portion of our citizens and our
students.

The nations population grew 10.2 percent from 1980 -
1990, growth rates of 11.7 percent of African-Americans, 38.7
percent for Native Americans, 104.7 percent for Asian American, and 52.8 percent of Latinos were considerably higher
(Hodgkinson, 1991). By 2010, 38 percent of the nation's youth
will be made up of African-Americans, Latinos, Native Americans and Asian Americans up from 30 percent in 1990.

Not only is there a substantial increase in the number of students from minority racial and ethnic groups including women, but there is also a larger number of students with special needs including not only those who may be physically challenged, but those who are challenged emotionally and learning wise as well. Our students are diverse not only in terms of their individual backgrounds but in terms of their specific cultures and subcultures. Recognizing and respecting these differences are important.

Why is all of this so important? As instructors, we must be sensitive to these changes. We must recognize that the techniques that used to work, the strategies we used to employ, the modes of instruction which once proved so effective, may not be so effective any more. As instructors of diverse populations, we must change our mind set and be willing to learn more about the varying cultures represented in our classes. We should be interested in investigating unique ways of instructing, willing to employ varied modes of instruction; paying close attention to individual learning styles and even cultural learning styles where appropiate.

This is a new time for education and we are explorers. Explorers are both bold and sensitive, bold enough to take daring new steps, yet sensitive enough to respond to their environments. Incorporating multicultural approaches to instruction is highly encouraged. Citing examples or using references which are not solely from a singular perspective or culture will help to make all class participants feel a part of the experience. To help create an environment of inclusion within your class these suggestions are offered. Keep in mind that multiculturalism supports the notion that there are many perspectives, or interpretations. Research clearly supports that the implementation of a multicultural cirriculum is uniquely and closely linked to teaching and learning.

Remember:
- Don't stereotype or assign rigid roles or attributes to a particular group when presenting issues.
- Attempt to show balance and selectivity in your course

materials (again being sensitive to your students)

- Attempt to show varied points of view when applicable.
- Attempt to capitalize on your students' experiences.
- Be receptive to new approaches.
- Research individual and cultural learning style theories.
- Be careful not to pigeonhole students. There are many exceptions to the rule.
- Diversity is not only reflected in culture, but is also reflected in gender, disability, and other reflections of difference.

Key Strategies for Better Instruction

- Learn the resources which are available to your students (use them).
- Awaken the interest of your students. Make them eager to pursue more knowledge. Be a spark plug, energizing your classroom.
- Help students solve real-life problems. Build their confidence.
- Supply students with sufficient opportunity for understanding the subject's fundamentals and basics.
- Enable students to develop an appropriately sensitive filter to screen out bad ideas and pass on good ones.
- Develop students' insight and feeling for a subject.
- Model appropriate behaviors and responses.
- Be willing to reach into the lives of your students.
- Appreciate your student's diversity. Celebrate and learn from it.
- Be patient with yourself. It will take time to learn new ways of approaching and solving these challenges. I urge you to be willing to try, for there is too much to be lost, if you don't.

Four key dimensions of teaching and learning have been

identified as having specific relevance to concerns of social and cultural diversity in the classroom.

They are presented here as an additional source of information to be considered as we create environments of inclusion in our classrooms, decreasing feelings of marginalization and increasing feelings of mattering experienced by many of our students.

Knowledge of the dimensions are vital as we make changes to accommodate our students and compliment their learning.

Students: Knowing and understanding the ways that students from various social and cultural backgrounds experience the classroom is key.

Instructor: Knowing ourselves as individuals with a prior history of academic socialization, interacting with a social and cultural background and learned beliefs is equally as vital.

Course Content: Creating a curriculum which incorporates diverse social and cultural perspectives should be a continuous goal in instruction.

Teaching Methods: Developing a wide repertoire of teaching methods to address the learning styles of students from varying backgrounds is necessary to aid learning.

Substantial research has urged instructors to actively involve students in the process of learning. The use of active learning strategies is encouraged. Many believe that all learning is active even when studetns simply listen. It is important to note that your students not only learn best while they only listen, but when they read, write, discuss and are engaged in solving problems. Being actively involved entails the use of higher order—thinking processes such as analysis, synthesis and evolution. Active learning has been defined as instructional activities which get students doing specific tasks and reflecting on those tasks.

Instruction Incorporating

Active learning has been shown to impact student achievement and mastery of course content at a greater level. Classroom instruction that incorporates greater discussions into lectures is one effective way to incorporate active learning into the classroom. Other strategies are also available to assist you in making adjustment to your instructional style to aid student learning, and I encourage you to research and implement them.

These suggestions may help to guide you as you adapt to the new challenges in the classroom. This is an exciting time to be involved in education. This is a time that demands that we address new challenges. How well we rise to meet the challenges at hand will not only determine our future, but the future of education as we know it.

The challenge is, at hand, good luck as you secure success and shape tomorrow.

SUMMARY

Far away, there in the sunshine, are my highest aspirations. I may not reach them, but I can look up and see their beauty, believe in them and try to follow where they lead."

Louisa May Alcott

The strategies contained in *Getting Real* have worked for many. It is my belief that they will work for you; use them. They will help you secure the success that you desire. Share them with others. It's vital to pass on information that works. The saying, "each *one, teach one,"* is most appropriate. Use this book as a reference. Review it as many times as necessary and make it a regular part of your study routine.

"I *think I can, I think I can!"* Wrong. "I *know I can. I know I can."* Don't be like *"the little engine that could"* and waste time procrastinating. Go for it! Set your goals realistically; make up your mind to reach them and achieve!

Until you make up your mind that you accept your goals as your own and are willing to sacrifice and work hard to achieve them, you will never be motivated to obtain them.

Motivation is not something someone gives you, it is a gift that you give to yourself. While it is true that others will try to motivate you to succeed, either you buy into it because it feels right for you, or you don't. Ultimately, it is up to you.

Listen to your heart, and if there is doubt, reassess your objectives, or talk it over with someone. You may find that your fears are keeping you from trying or that the goal isn't right for you. Either way, at least you won't waste time on something you don't really want.

Once you've set the goal and it is yours, be determined to climb the highest mountain. If you slide down, pick yourself up, and keep on climbing. Be resilient and be determined. People will see this as a measure of your motivation and determination.

Once the determination is set, you will be motivated to use whatever resources are available to assist you. You have been introduced to a wide range of techniques which are designed to help you reach your definition of success. If you take the time to master the principles suggested—you will increase your chances for excellence both academically and personally.

Practice these techniques over and over so that they become "weapons" in your arsenal of success skills. Use combinations of techniques to refine your style, accepting and incorporating what works best for you.

I believe that being a successful student requires setting goals, developing determination to achieve them, and using the resources that are available to you. It does not mean that every battle is won, but rather that one tries.

Commit now, us this material to aid in your achievement. Your success can be a reality.

"Success is only a goal away."

Alicia's Philosophy

There is no secret to success. It requires hard work, sacrifice and determination. It requires setting your sights on an objective and relentlessly pursuing it. If your goal is success and you have prepared yourself adequately, achievement of the goal can be realized.

Greatness lies within each of us. Discovering and sharing this greatness is imperative. Always remember that there are people who care about you and want to help you succeed. Your family, instructors, counselors, and friends all have a stake in your achievement and want it to become reality. Be gracious and always thank those who cared enough to lift you up and to support your endeavors. By reading this book, you have laid the ground work; now the rest is up to you to incorporate these strategies.

You deserve success. Now earn it! Prepare as winners do, and achieve as I know you will.

Here's To You and Excellence . . . My best to you, and achieving the success connection. I wish you good things always.

Alicia

About the Author

Alicia B. Harvey-Smith is currently the Executive Director of Student Development at The Baltimore City Community College. She not only directs campus counseling efforts for a multi-faceted center which includes: Career Exploration and Development, Job Placement, Transfer/Articulation, Crisis Intervention Programs, Unique Specialized Support Groups, Retention Programming, Academic Advising for Developmental and Probationary Students, Single Parent Programs, Peer Counseling, but is directly responsible for overseeing the disabled students services office, student support services, complete student services at a second campus and intercollegiate athletics.

Prior to this she coordinated the College Success Seminar Program at Burlington County College in Pemberton, N.J. She has instructed at the middle school, secondary and college levels in the areas of Special Education, Freshman Seminar and English, as well as for the U.S. Military in the areas of Basic Skills Education and Financial Management.

Holding several professional memberships, awards, and honors, Alicia is most proud of her involvements with The American Association of Women in Community Colleges, The National Institute of Leadership Development, and The National Council on Student Development for which she is an Executive Board member, Region III Representative and co-editor of its national newsletter.

Appointed by the Executive Board of NCSD to a national commission of the American Association of Community Colleges to study academic and student ran community development. Alicia is exposed to key issues affecting students throughout the country. Recognized as an up and coming leader in Higher Education and the Student Development field, she has been cited in *Who's Who Among All American Women, Who's Who In American Education,* and *Who's Who of Women Executives.*

Her articles have been published in *The Community College Times, American Association of Women In Community College Journal, National Council of Black American Affairs Newsletter* and *The National Council of Student Development newsletters,* and is a contributing author for *Nests for Dreams, Backdrops for Visions: Making a Difference With Students,* edited by Becherer and Becherer. Alicia is a member of the National Institute of Leadership Development—International Leaders Program for Women—who are innovative on community college campuses. She is frequently asked to lecture at a variety of forums, and enjoys topics which empower, motivate, educate and elevate.

Alicia is excited to lend her voice to the student development professionals across the country striving to make systemic change, by creating quality holistic student support programs for diverse student populations, and providing students with real solutions to the challenges they face. She is currently a Ph.D. candidate in the University of Maryland's Counseling and Personnel Services Program with an emphasis in Student Development and Retention.

She resides in Baltimore County with her husband Donald.